Words
for
New Readers

HarperCollins*Publishers*

Part of this dictionary is also published under the title *My First Picture Dictionary*.

D'Nealian is the registered trademark of Donald Neal Thurber.

First HarperCollins edition published 1991

Illustration and photograph credits appear on page 311.

Library of Congress Cataloging-in-Publication Data

Words for new readers.—1st HarperCollins ed.
  p. cm.
  Summary: An alphabetically arranged list of words, each defined by a picture and an illustrative sentence.
  ISBN 0-06-275008-9
  1. Picture dictionaries, English—Juvenile literature.
  [1. Picture dictionaries.]
  PE 1629.W6   1990
  423'.1—dc20   90-5073

Library of Congress Catalog Card Number 90-5073

ISBN 0-06-275008-9

45678910-WEB-999897969594

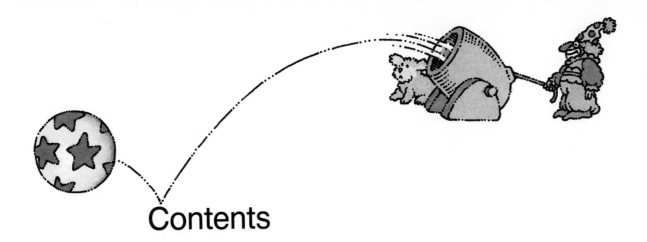

Contents

Introduction   4
How to Read an Entry   5
Your Picture Dictionary   6–298
Find Out the Facts!   299
    Shapes   299
    Numbers, Measurement   300
    Time   301
    Parts of the Body   302
    Healthy Snacks   303
    Finding Places - Maps   304
        The United States
        Countries of the World
        Continents
    Calendar   306
    Holidays   307
    Opposites   308
    Colors   310
Credits   311
The D'Nealian® Alphabet   312

Introduction

Words for New Readers is an attractive and colorful book of words and pictures for beginning readers and writers. It is designed for those children who have advanced beyond the picture-book level, and introduces them to the idea of using a reference book. *Words for New Readers* prepares children for an actual dictionary by familiarizing them with simple dictionary skills.

The words in the book are listed in alphabetical order. *Words for New Readers* is, then, best suited for children who know the alphabet and have had some experience alphabetizing letters and words. Each entry word is listed in large, heavy type. A simple definition is given for each entry word. The entry word is then used in a sentence.

Most of the words in *Words for New Readers* are illustrated. Original art, photographs, cartoons, and fine art are used to picture the word being defined. A caption, always the same as the entry word for easy reference, accompanies each illustration.

The 1500 entries in *Words for New Readers* were chosen from a list of words that children will encounter in school and at home. Numerous books for beginning readers (including reading, language arts, handwriting, science, health, mathematics, and social studies texts) were read and their vocabulary was analyzed to make up this word list. Names of things children commonly encounter in their homes and neighborhoods are also included.

At the back of the book is a section called "Find Out the Facts!" Its colorfully illustrated pages contain useful information on shapes, the human body, nutrition, maps, numbers, measurement, telling time, the calendar, holidays, opposites, and colors.

Scott, Foresman and Company has been a leader in producing quality children's dictionaries for more than fifty years. *Words for New Readers* was prepared by an experienced team of editors, designers, and illustrators. Throughout its development and production, a panel of primary teachers served as project advisers.

People use dictionaries throughout their entire lifetime. Gaining access to the information contained in dictionaries is therefore an important learning experience. In using *Words for New Readers,* young children take the first steps toward acquiring basic dictionary skills.

On the inside back cover we have suggested some activities to help your child use this book to learn about words. We hope your child will spend many happy hours with *Words for New Readers.*

The Editors

How to Read an Entry

Several sample entries are printed below.
Explanations of the parts of an entry
appear in the boxes.

The entry word is in a separate column so it is easy to find. It is printed in heavy black type. It shows you how the word is spelled.

The small raised number tells you that two different entry words with different meanings have the same spelling.

A sentence shows how the word is used.

A sentence tells you the meaning of the word.

A picture helps to show the meaning of the word. Each picture has a caption that is the same as the entry word.

top¹ Top means the highest part. We saw the **top** of the mountain. **tops.**

top¹

top² A top is a toy that spins. The **top** went round and round. **tops.**

top²

A number is printed before each meaning of a word when more than one meaning is given.

trip **1.** When you go on a **trip**, you travel from one place to another. Let's take a **trip** to the ocean. **trips.**
2. Trip also means to fall. I tripped on the rope. **tripped, tripping.**

true True means right or correct. It is **true** that 4 and 6 are 10. A **true** story is not made up. **truer, truest.**

Word endings and special forms of entry words come at the end of the entry. They are printed in heavy black type.

A a

a　Pat has **a** red hat. Do you have **a** book on cats? Thanksgiving comes once **a** year.

able　If you are **able** to do something, it means that you can do it. Jan is **able** to walk on her hands.

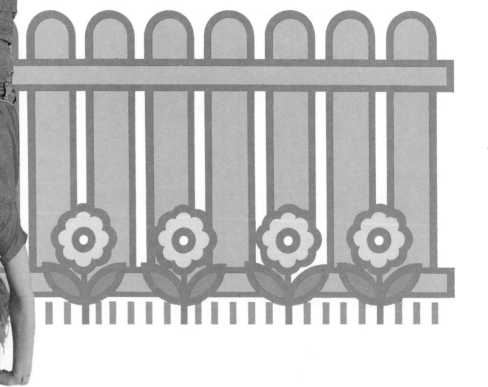

able

about   I like stories **about** animals. Bob and Sue are **about** the same size. I have **about** finished my homework.

above   The red bird is on the branch **above** the blue bird.

above

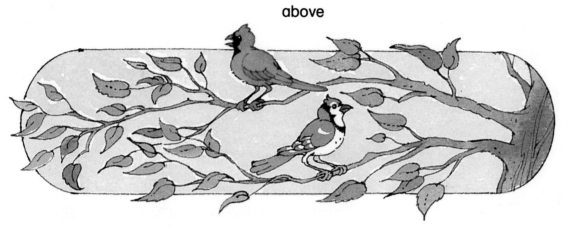

across   Maria walked **across** the street to play with her friends.

act   Act means to pretend you are someone else. Lee **acted** the part of the wolf in the play. **acted, acting.**

act

add   Add means to put things together. When you **add**, you find how much or how many. She **added** 2 and 3 to make 5. **added, adding.**

adult   An **adult** is a grown-up person. Your teacher is an **adult. adults.**

adult

A a

after The dog ran **after** the ball. Five comes **after** four.

after

afternoon Afternoon is the part of day between morning and evening. We played ball this **afternoon** after school. **afternoons.**

again When you do something once more, you do it **again.** Beth tried **again** and got the right answer.

again

age Your **age** is the number of years you have lived. Sam started school at the **age** of five.

ahead

ahead The girl in red was **ahead** of all the other runners. Go **ahead** with your work.

air The **air** we breathe is all around us. It has no smell, taste, or color. The **air** above us is called the sky.

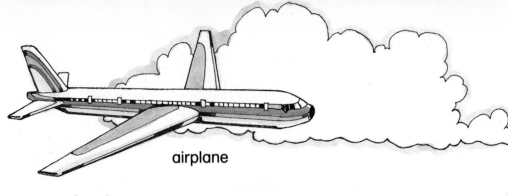

airplane

airplane An **airplane** is a machine that can fly. **Airplanes** have wings and engines. **airplanes.**

airport

airport An **airport** is a place where airplanes land and take off. **airports.**

alike When things are **alike**, they are like one another. When things are **alike**, they are not different. The twins look **alike**.

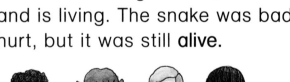

alike

alive When something is **alive**, it has life and is living. The snake was badly hurt, but it was still **alive**.

       all

all All the children are smiling. The mice ate **all** the cheese.

alligator An **alligator** is a large animal with thick skin. It has a very large mouth and a long tail. **Alligators** live in warm rivers. **alligators.**

alligator

A | a

almost

alone

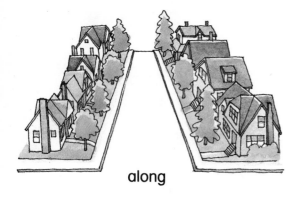

along

alphabet

almost   I **almost** missed the bus. It is **almost** ten o'clock.

alone   **Alone** means without anyone else. He sat **alone** because he didn't know the other children.

along   Trees are planted **along** the street. We took our dog **along**.

alphabet   The **alphabet** is all the letters from A to Z. Can you say the **alphabet**?

already   She has **already** read this book. Her father said she had **already** left for school.

also   Sam has a dog, but he likes cats **also**.

always   Always eat a good breakfast before you go to school.

am   Today I **am** seven years old.

amount   The **amount** of something is how much there is or how many there are. The **amount** of milk Jan needs for the soup is one cup. One dollar is a small **amount** of money. **amounts.**

amount

an   There is **an** apple in the basket, and a banana too. I ate **an** egg and two pieces of toast.

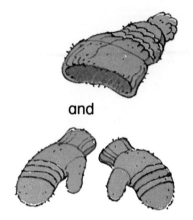

and

and   His hat **and** mittens are blue. 4 **and** 2 make 6. Sue **and** Lee played a game.

angry   When you are upset and not pleased about something, you are **angry**. Dad was **angry** when I broke the window. **angrier, angriest.**

angry

A a

animal   Any living thing that can move about is an **animal. Animals** cannot make their own food from sunlight as plants do. People, dogs, birds, fish, ants, and worms are **animals. animals.**

animal

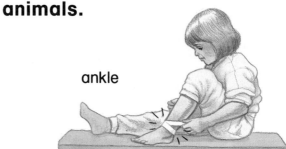

ankle

ankle   The **ankle** is the part of the body between the foot and leg. She fell and hurt her **ankle. ankles.**

another   She ate **another** apple. The cap didn't fit, so I chose **another.**

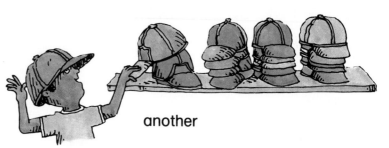

another

answer   **Answer** means to speak or write something when someone asks a question. He **answered** the question. **answered, answering.**

ant   An **ant** is a small insect. **Ants** live in the ground. Many **ants** live together in a group. **ants.**

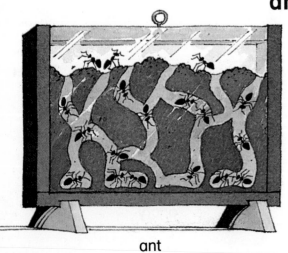

ant

any   Choose **any** toy you like. Are there **any** cookies left?

apartment   An **apartment** is a group of rooms to live in. They live in a small **apartment** in that building. **apartments.**

apartment

ape   An **ape** is a large animal with long arms and no tail. **Apes** can stand almost straight and can walk on two feet. A gorilla is an **ape. apes.**

ape

apple   An **apple** is a fruit that grows on trees. **Apples** are red, yellow, or green. **apples.**

apple

aquarium   An **aquarium** is a place where fish and other water animals are kept. Some **aquariums** are glass bowls or boxes. Others are buildings where you can see many kinds of water animals. **aquariums.**

aquarium

A | a

area

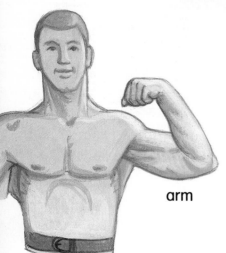
arm

are   You **are** right. We **are** ready. They **are** waiting for us.

area   The **area** of something is the amount of space it covers. A large **area** of the earth is covered by water. The dining **area** is where we eat. **areas.**

arm   The **arm** is the part of the body between the shoulder and the hand. **arms.**

around

around   The top spun **around.** There was a white fence **around** the yard.

art

art   Paintings and drawings are kinds of **art.** The teacher showed the children's **art** to their parents.

artist

artist   An **artist** is a person who makes paintings and drawings. **artists.**

as   Jane ran **as** fast **as** she could to win the race.

ask   **1.** **Ask** means to try to find out something. We had to **ask** the way to the monkey house.
2. **Ask** also means to invite someone. Tom **asked** six friends to his party. **asked, asking.**

ask

asleep   When you are **asleep** you rest your body and your mind. Jim tried to stay awake, but he fell **asleep.**

asleep

astronaut   An **astronaut** rides in a spaceship. **Astronauts** landed on the moon. **astronauts.**

astronaut

A | a

at

at The boy is **at** the chalkboard. The dog barked **at** the cat.

ate We **ate** our lunch in the park.

ate

attic

attic An **attic** is a space in a house just below the roof. It is above the other rooms. We store things in our **attic**. **attics.**

aunt Your **aunt** is your father's sister or your mother's sister. Your uncle's wife is also your **aunt. aunts.**

author   An **author** is a person who writes books, stories, poems, or plays. Who is your favorite **author**? **authors.**

author

automobile   An **automobile** is a machine that people ride in. It has a motor and four wheels. Another word for **automobile** is car. **automobiles.**

automobile

autumn   Autumn is one of the four seasons. It comes after summer and before winter. The leaves fall from the trees in **autumn.** Another name for **autumn** is fall.

autumn

awake   Awake means not asleep. We were **awake** in time to see the sun rise.

away   The dog ran **away** from the bear. Jan put the game **away.** They will be **away** for a week.

awake

Bb

baby A baby is a very young child. Little babies can't walk. **babies.**

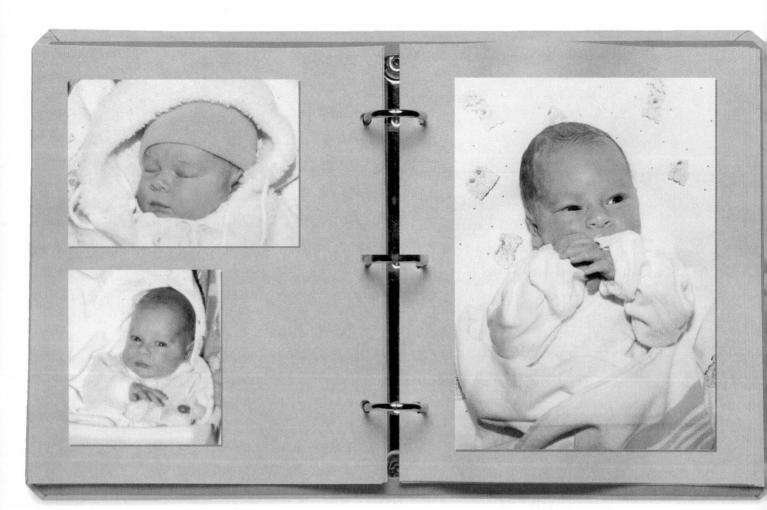

baby

back The part of the body opposite the chest and stomach is the **back**. **backs.**

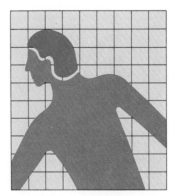
back

bad Bad means not good or not right. That medicine tastes **bad.** That **bad** dog ate my lunch. Ann has a **bad** cold. **worse, worst.**

bad   worse   worst

bag A **bag** holds things. **Bags** can be made of paper, plastic, or other things. **bags.**

bag

bake Bake means to cook something in an oven. Tom helped Grandpa **bake** a cake. **baked, baking.**

baker A **baker** makes and sells bread, pies, and cakes. **bakers.**

baker

19

B | b

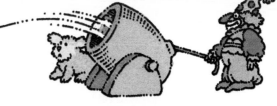

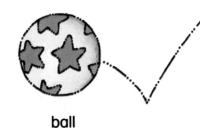

ball A **ball** is round and is used to play games. You can throw a **ball** or bounce it. Jane kicked the **ball** to John. **balls.**

ball

balloon A **balloon** is a toy. It is made of thin rubber filled with air. **balloons.**

banana

banana A **banana** is a curved, yellow fruit. Bananas grow in bunches on trees. **bananas.**

bank

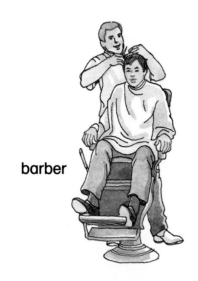

barber

bank A **bank** is a place where people keep their money. A **bank** can be a building where people work. A **bank** can be a box or jar to save pennies in. **banks.**

barber A **barber** is a person who cuts hair. **barbers.**

bark[1]

bark[1] Bark covers the outside of a tree. It covers the trunk and branches.

bark² A **bark** is the sound that a dog makes. The dog's loud **bark** made me jump. **barks.**

barn

barn A **barn** is a farm building. It is used to store food for animals. Cows and horses are kept in the **barn** at night. **barns.**

baseball 1. Baseball is a game played with a ball and bat. 2. A **baseball** is also the name of the ball used in this game. **baseballs.**

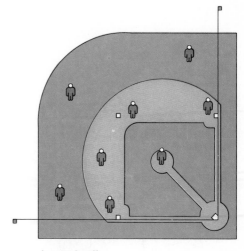

baseball

basket A **basket** is used to hold things. A **basket** can be big or little. **baskets.**

basket

basketball 1. Basketball is a game played with a large ball. Players have to throw the ball through a ring. 2. A **basketball** is also the name of the ball used in this game. **basketballs.**

basketball

B | b

bat¹   A **bat** is used to hit the ball in baseball. **bats.**

bat¹

bat²

bat²   A **bat** is a small animal that flies. Its face is like that of a mouse. Its wings are covered with skin. Bats fly around at night. **bats.**

bath   When you take a **bath** you wash your body. The baby splashes when Mom gives him a **bath**. **baths.**

bathing suit   You wear a **bathing suit** when you go swimming. **bathing suits.**

bathing suit

bathtub   A **bathtub** is a tub to take a bath in. She filled the **bathtub** with water. **bathtubs.**

bathtub

be   He wants to **be** an artist when he grows up. Will Sue and Joe **be** at the party?

beach   A **beach** is an area of land next to the water. **Beaches** are covered with sand or stones. **beaches.**

beach

bean   A **bean** is a vegetable. **Beans** grow on vines. There are string **beans**, lima **beans**, and kidney beans. **beans.**

bear   A **bear** is a large animal with thick fur. Many **bears** sleep most of the winter. **bears.**

bean

bear

beautiful

beautiful   **Beautiful** means that something we see or hear is very pretty. We saw a **beautiful** rainbow. That was a **beautiful** song.

B b

beaver

beaver A **beaver** is an animal with soft fur and large front teeth. It has a wide, flat tail. **Beavers** cut down trees with their teeth. They live both in water and on land. **beavers.**

became The puppy soon **became** a big dog.

became

because The game was called off **because** it rained.

become This small plant will **become** a tree. It is winter, and **becoming** colder. **became, becoming.**

bed

bed A **bed** is something to sleep on. What time do you go to **bed**? Mom put the baby in her **bed**. **beds.**

bedroom

B|b

bedroom A **bedroom** is a room to sleep in. Tom and Bob share a **bedroom**. **bedrooms.**

bee A **bee** is an insect that can fly. **Bees** make honey. Some **bees** live in large groups. **bees.**

bee

been You can tell that Jan and Joe have **been** playing in the mud. Have you **been** to the circus?

beetle A **beetle** is an insect. Its shiny front wings cover its back wings when it is not flying. **beetles.**

beetle

before Your turn comes **before** mine. Have you been to the zoo **before**?

began It **began** to snow.

begin **Begin** means to start. When did it **begin** to snow? The race is going to begin. **began, begun, beginning.**

begin

B | b

begun   The wind has **begun** to blow.

behind   The band marched **behind** the leader.

behind

bell

being   The dog is **being** fed.

bell   A **bell** makes a ringing sound. Sue rang the front door **bell**. Some **bells** make a pretty sound when you shake them. **bells.**

belong   Do these mittens **belong** to you?

below

below   The blue bird is on the branch **below** the red bird.

belt A **belt** is a strip of cloth or leather. You wear a **belt** around your waist. **belts.**

belt

bend If you **bend** something, you make it curved or crooked. The strong man said he would **bend** the piece of iron. **bent, bending.**

bent He **bent** the iron into a curve.

bent

berry A **berry** is a small, juicy fruit with seeds. Strawberries and raspberries are **berries**. **berries.**

berry

beside They camped **beside** the river. The girl was reading with her dog **beside** her.

beside

B | b

best His work is good. Your work is better, but her work is **best**.

good   better   best

better Sue's picture is good, but I think Pat's is **better**.

between The boy stood **between** two tall men.

bicycle A **bicycle** has two wheels. You ride it by pushing the pedals. **bicycles.**

between

bicycle

big If something is **big**, it has great size. Something **big** is not little. Jerry has a **big** dog. Lita's dog is **bigger** than Jerry's. It is the **biggest** I have ever seen. **bigger, biggest.**

big   bigger

bike Bike is another word for bicycle. **bikes.**

bill A bill is part of a bird's mouth. It is hard and comes to a point. **bills.**

bill

bird A bird is an animal that has feathers, wings, and two legs. Most birds can fly. Robins, eagles, and ducks are birds. **birds.**

bird

birthday A birthday is the day on which a person is born. Birthdays can be happy days. **birthdays.**

birthday

bit He bit into the apple.

bite

bite When you bite something, you cut it with your teeth. If you bite the apple, you should finish eating it. **bit, bitten, biting.**

B | b

bitten

bitten   Someone has **bitten** this apple!

black   **Black** is a color. The words in this book are printed in **black**.

blanket

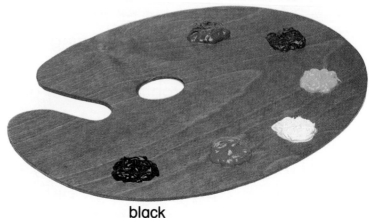
black

blanket   A **blanket** keeps you warm. Some **blankets** are soft and fluffy. I have a blue **blanket** on my bed. **blankets.**

blew   The wind **blew** the leaves all over the yard.

block   **1.** A **block** is a thick piece of wood or plastic. My little sister built a house with her blocks. **blocks.**
2. **Block** also means to fill so that nothing can pass. A big truck **blocked** the street. **blocked, blocking.**

block

blow

blow   Blow means to move air quickly. A strong wind started to **blow**. Anna helped Nan **blow** up balloons. **blew, blown, blowing.**

blown   The wind has **blown** Bob's hat off.

blue   Blue is a color. On a clear day the sky is **blue**.

blue

boat   A **boat** is something to ride in on the water. We crossed the lake in a boat. **boats.**

boat

body   Your **body** is your whole person, from head to toe. People and animals have **bodies**. **bodies.**

body

B|b

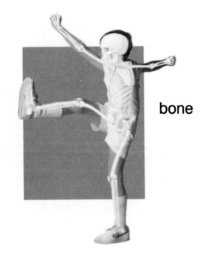
bone

bone A **bone** is the hard inside support that helps protect your body. **Bones** help you move. There are over 200 **bones** under your skin. **bones.**

book A **book** has sheets of paper inside two covers. The pages in this **book** have writing and pictures on them. **books.**

book

boot

boot A **boot** is a covering for the foot and leg. **Boots** keep your feet and legs dry. We wear **boots** in the rain or snow. **boots.**

bottle A **bottle** can hold milk or juice. **Bottles** are made of glass or plastic. Most **bottles** have caps on them. **bottles.**

bottle

bottom The **bottom** is the lowest part of anything. Jack held the **bottom** of the ladder as Mom climbed to the top. **bottoms.**

bought   He **bought** a new pair of shoes.

bounce   If you throw a ball against a wall it will **bounce** back to you. **Bounce** means to spring back after hitting something. **bounced, bouncing.**

bounce

bow¹   When you **bow** you bend your head or body. The actors **bowed** when the people clapped. **bowed, bowing.** Bow¹ sounds like how.

bow¹

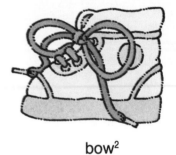

bow²

bow²   A **bow** is a special kind of knot. You make a **bow** when you tie your shoe. **bows.** Bow² sounds like so.

bowl   A bowl is a deep dish. Jane ate a **bowl** of soup for lunch. **bowls.**

bowl

B b

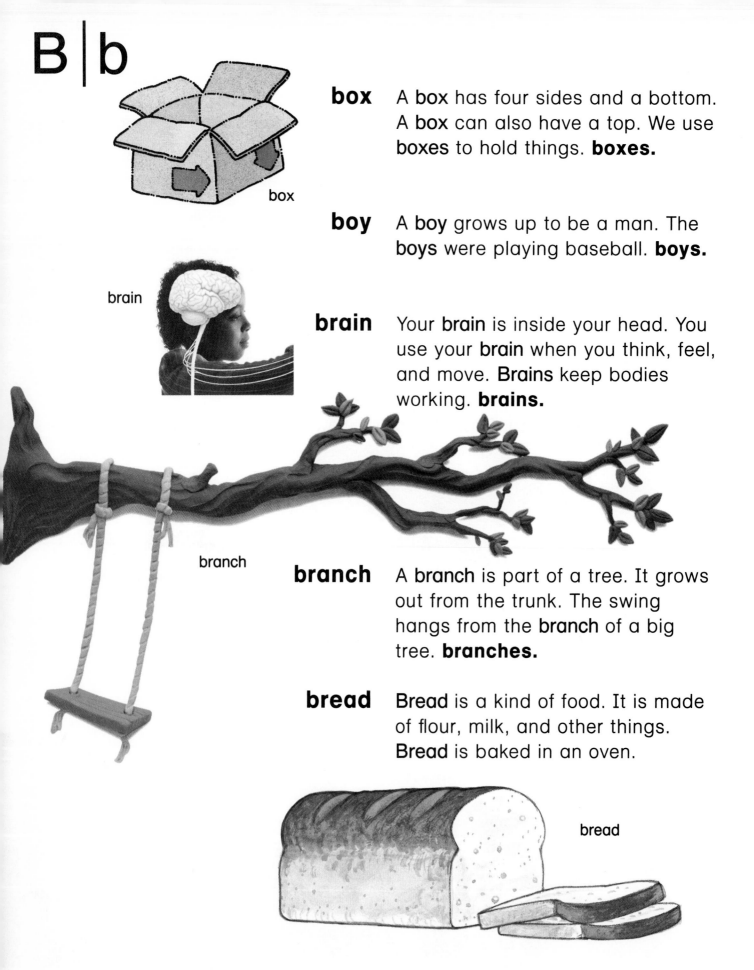

box A **box** has four sides and a bottom. A **box** can also have a top. We use **boxes** to hold things. **boxes.**

box

boy A **boy** grows up to be a man. The **boys** were playing baseball. **boys.**

brain

brain Your **brain** is inside your head. You use your **brain** when you think, feel, and move. **Brains** keep bodies working. **brains.**

branch

branch A **branch** is part of a tree. It grows out from the trunk. The swing hangs from the **branch** of a big tree. **branches.**

bread **Bread** is a kind of food. It is made of flour, milk, and other things. **Bread** is baked in an oven.

bread

34

break If you **break** something it comes apart or goes to pieces. You might **break** a glass bottle if you drop it. **broke, broken, breaking.**

break

breakfast **Breakfast** is a meal eaten in the morning. We had cereal for **breakfast** today. **breakfasts.**

breathe You **breathe** air through your nose or mouth. You **breathe** air in and then you **breathe** air out. **breathed, breathing.**

brick

brick A **brick** is hard and heavy. **Bricks** are used to build houses and walls. **bricks.**

bridge A **bridge** is a road built over water. We walked across the **bridge** to the other side of the river. **bridges.**

bridge

35

B | b

bright

bright   Something that is **bright** gives much light. Something that shines is **bright**. A new penny is **bright**. The sun is **brighter** than the stars. **brighter, brightest.**

bring   **Bring** means to carry something to another place. Please **bring** me a glass of water. **brought, bringing.**

broke   Lee dropped the flower pot and it **broke**.

broke

broken

broken   He tried to fix the **broken** flower pot.

broom   A **broom** is a brush with a long handle. Lee's mother used a **broom** to sweep the floor. **brooms.**

broom

brother   Your **brother** is a boy who has the same mother and father that you have. Sam has a big **brother** and a little sister. **brothers.**

brought

brought   Ann's friends **brought** presents to her birthday party.

brown   Brown is a color. Toast and chocolate are **brown**.

brown

brush   A **brush** is made of stiff hairs or plastic. There are many kinds of **brushes**. You use a **brush** to paint a house. **brushes.**

brush

bud   A **bud** is a small bump on a plant. A **bud** will grow into a flower or a leaf. **buds.**

bug   A **bug** is anything that crawls or flies like an insect. A **bug** can be an ant, a fly, or a spider. **bugs.**

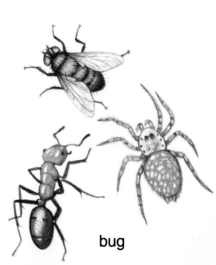

bug

B | b

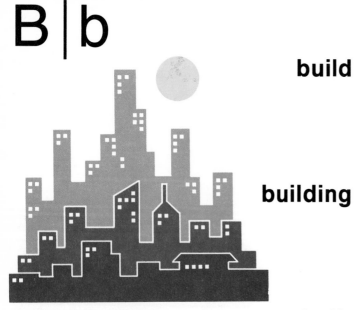

building

burn

build   When you **build** something, you put things together. Dave can **build** a house with these blocks. **built, building.**

building   A **building** has walls and a roof. Schools, houses, and barns are **buildings**. It took many people to build that big **building**. **buildings.**

built   They **built** their house of brick. The fence is **built** of wood.

burn   **Burn** means to be on fire. The campfire **burned** brightly. **burned, burning.**

bus

bus   A **bus** is like a big car with many seats. A **bus** carries people from place to place. A school **bus** takes children to school. **buses.**

bush A **bush** is a plant smaller than a tree. A **bush** has branches that start near the ground. Some **bushes** have flowers, and some have fruit. **bushes.**

bush

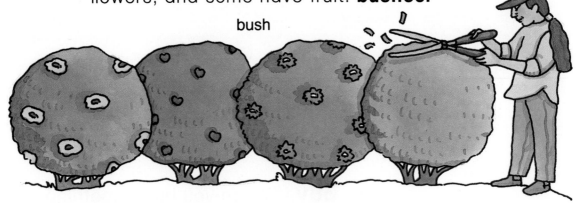

busy When you are **busy** you have a lot to do. The children are **busy** painting a playhouse. They are the **busiest** children I've ever seen. **busier, busiest.**

busy

but You may look at the flowers, **but** you must not pick them. We wanted to go swimming **but** we couldn't.

butter Butter is a soft yellow food. It is made from cream. Tom spreads **butter** on his toast.

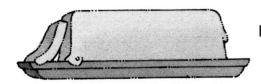

butter

butterfly A **butterfly** is an insect. It has two pairs of wings with bright colors. Some caterpillars change into butterflies. **butterflies.**

butterfly

B b

button

button A **button** is used to hold clothes together. Some shirts have **buttons** down the front. **buttons.**

buy When you **buy** something, you pay money for it. Ruth wanted to **buy** a toy car. **bought, buying.**

buy

buzz Buzz means to make a humming sound. Bees and flies **buzz.** **buzzed, buzzing.**

by The playground is **by** the school. The tree house was built **by** Ann and her friends.

by

SCHOOL

Cc

cab   A **cab** is a car with a driver. The driver is paid to take people places. **cabs.**

cactus   A **cactus** is a plant that grows in hot, dry places. Cactuses are covered with sharp points. **cactuses.**

cactus

C c

cage A **cage** is a place to keep birds or wild animals. **Cages** have bars or wires. **cages.**

cage

cake **Cake** is a sweet food made of flour, sugar, eggs, and other things. We baked a **cake** for Bob's birthday. **cakes.**

calculator

calculator A **calculator** is used to find the answers to number problems. **calculators.**

calendar A **calendar** is a kind of chart. **Calendars** show the months, weeks, and days of the year. **calendars.**

calendar

calf A **calf** is a baby cow. **calves.**

calf

call   **1.** Call means to shout or say something in a loud voice. He **called** to the bus driver to wait.
2. Call also means to give a name to someone or something. They **call** their dog King. **called, calling.**

calves   We saw a cow and two **calves.**

came   He **came** to the party early.

camel   A **camel** is a large animal that can carry heavy loads. **Camels** can go a long time without water. **camels.**

camel

camera   A **camera** is used to take pictures or movies. **cameras.**

camera

camp   A **camp** is a group of tents or huts where people live for a time. Many children go to summer **camps.** **camps.**

camp

43

C | c

can¹ Can you come to the party tomorrow night? She **can** sing and dance. **could.**

can²

can² A **can** is used to hold something. We buy food, paint, and fruit juice in **cans. cans.**

candle

candle A **candle** is a stick of wax with a string in the center. It gives light as it burns. Kim's birthday cake had six **candles. candles.**

candy Candy is a sweet food made of sugar or syrup. Chocolate, fruit, and nuts are often added to **candy. candies.**

candy

cannot Jean **cannot** come to the birthday party tomorrow.

cap   A cap is a kind of hat. Caps are soft and fit the head closely. Tom wore a blue cap. **caps.**

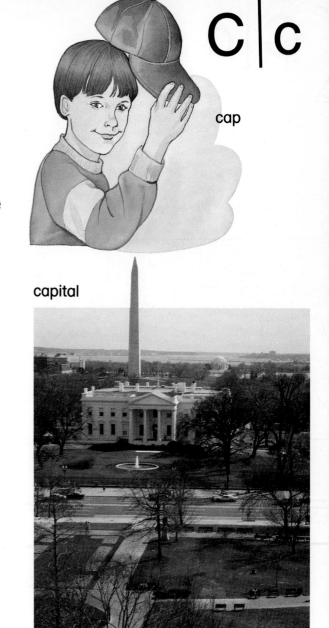

cap

capital   **1.** A capital is a city where a country's or state's leaders work. Washington, D.C., is the **capital** of the United States.
2. Capital also means A, B, C, D, or any other large letter. **capitals.**

capital

car   A car is a machine that people ride in. It has a motor and four wheels. Another word for car is automobile. **cars.**

card   A card is a flat piece of thick paper. A birthday card, a library card, and a report card are different kinds of cards. **cards.**

card

45

C | c

care 1. You take **care** of someone when you look after that person. Grandmother took **care** of me.
2. **Care** also means to feel interest in something. He **cares** more about cars than anything else. **cared, caring.**

careful Being **careful** means thinking about what you say or do. Be **careful** with your new bicycle.

carpenter

carpenter A **carpenter** builds things out of wood. **Carpenters** build and fix the wooden parts of houses and boats. **carpenters.**

carrot

carrot A **carrot** is a long, orange vegetable. **Carrots** grow under the ground. **carrots.**

carry **Carry** means to take something from one place to another. Jim **carried** the bags to the kitchen. **carried, carrying.**

carry

castle   A **castle** is a large stone building with thick walls. Many years ago, kings and queens lived in **castles. castles.**

castle

cat   A **cat** is a small animal with soft fur. **Cats** are often kept as pets. **cats.**

cat

catch   **Catch** means to take and hold something moving. **Catch** the football with both hands. **caught, catching.**

caterpillar   A **caterpillar** is an insect. Most **caterpillars** are furry and bright in color. Some **caterpillars** change into butterflies. **caterpillars.**

caterpillar

cattle   **Cattle** are animals raised for milk and meat. Cows are **cattle.**

cattle

47

C c

caught

cave

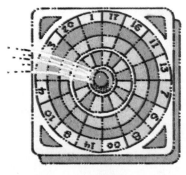

center

cent

caught   When I threw the ball, Mary **caught** it.

cause   **Cause** means to make something happen. The fire **caused** much damage. **caused, causing.**

cave   A **cave** is an empty space under the ground. Most **caves** have an opening in the side of a hill or mountain. **caves.**

cavity   A **cavity** is a hole. The dentist filled two **cavities** in my teeth. **cavities.**

cent   A **cent** is a kind of money. It is also called a penny. There are one hundred **cents** in a dollar. **cents.**

center   **Center** means the middle of something. She hit the **center** of the board and won the game.

centimeter   A **centimeter** is used to measure how long something is. This line is one **centimeter** long ____ . **centimeters.**

cereal   **Cereal** is a food made from corn, rice, or other grains. Many people eat **cereal** with milk for breakfast. **cereals.**

cereal

chair

chair   A **chair** is a seat with a back and legs. Tom sat in the **chair** by the window. **chairs.**

chalk   **Chalk** is used to write or draw. The teacher used a piece of **chalk** to write her name.

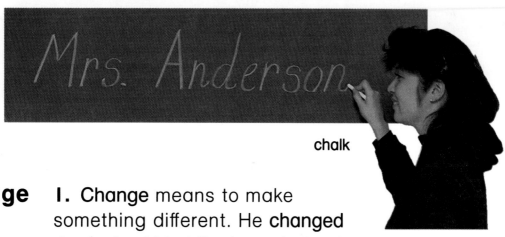
chalk

change   **1.** **Change** means to make something different. He **changed** the look of his bike by painting it. **changed, changing.**
2. **Change** also means money you get back. The bus driver gave me ten cents in **change.**

C c

chart

chart A **chart** is a list or drawing that shows facts. Sara made a **chart** showing the weather each day of last week. **charts.**

check 1. **Check** means to make sure something is true or right. **Check** your answers. **checked, checking.** 2. A **check** is a mark (√) that shows something is true or right. **checks.**

cheek

cheek The **cheek** is the part of the face just below the eye. His **cheeks** are red. **cheeks.**

cheer

cheer **Cheer** means to call out or yell loudly to show you like something. Let's **cheer** for our team. **cheered, cheering.**

cheese **Cheese** is a food made from milk. We often eat **cheese** for lunch. **cheeses.**

cheese

cherry A cherry is a small, red fruit. Cherries grow on trees and are round and juicy. **cherries.**

cherry

chest The front part of the body between the neck and the stomach is the chest. **chests.**

chest

chew Chew means to crush with the teeth. Chew your meat well. **chewed, chewing.**

chick

chicken

chick A chick is a young chicken. **chicks.**

chicken A chicken is a bird raised for food. **chickens.**

C c

child A **child** is a young boy or young girl. **Children** grow up to be men and women. **children.**

children

children **Children** are young boys and girls.

chin

chin The **chin** is the part of the face below the mouth. **chins.**

chocolate **Chocolate** is a food made from the seeds of a tree. It tastes good and is used to make candy.

choose

choose **Choose** means to pick out from a group. Karen often **chooses** books about animals, while Sue **chooses** books about flying. **chose, chosen, choosing.**

chose John **chose** to see the movie about astronauts.

chosen Sue was **chosen** to lead the parade.

church A **church** is a place where some people go to pray. **churches.**

church

circle **1.** A **circle** is a shape like a round line. Flowers grew in a **circle** around the tree. **circles.**
2. Circle also means to go around something. He **circled** the school on his bike. **circled, circling.**

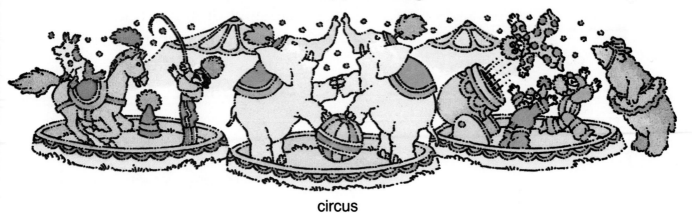
circus

circus A **circus** is a traveling show. A **circus** has clowns, horses, and wild animals. **circuses.**

city

city A **city** is a large town. Many people live and work in a **city. Cities** often have tall buildings. **cities.**

C | c

clap

clap   Clap means to hit the hands together to make a sound. We **clapped** when the show was over. **clapped, clapping.**

classify

class   A class is a group of boys and girls who learn together. Most schools have many **classes**. **classes.**

classify   Classify means to put in order by group. Jim likes to **classify** dinosaurs into meat eaters and plant eaters. **classified, classifying.**

classroom

classroom   A classroom is a room in which classes are held. **classrooms.**

clay

clay   Clay is a kind of earth. Wet **clay** can be shaped into pots and dishes. **Clay** gets hard when it dries.

clean

clean 1. **Clean** means free from dirt. Mom is proud of her **clean** car. **cleaner, cleanest.**
2. **Clean** also means to make free from dirt. **Clean** your boots. **cleaned, cleaning.**

clear 1. **Clear** means easy to see through. I saw my cat through the **clear** glass.
2. **Clear** also means bright or without clouds. On **clear** days the children went swimming. **clearer, clearest.**

clear

climb **Climb** means to go up something. We **climbed** the stairs. Sue **climbs** trees. **climbed, climbing.**

clock A **clock** shows what time it is. The hands of the **clock** showed it was almost noon. **clocks.**

clock

C | c

close   Close means to shut. Close the window of your bedroom. **closed, closing.**

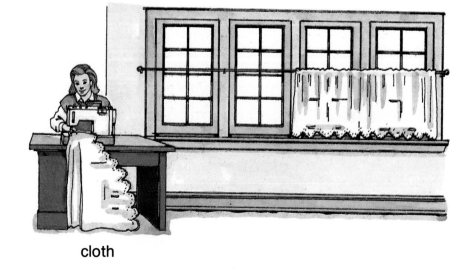
cloth

clothes

cloth   Cloth is used to make clothes and other things. Mom made curtains out of blue **cloth.**

clothes   Clothes cover the body. Dresses, pants, sweaters, and shirts are clothes.

clothing   Clothing is another word for clothes.

cloud   A cloud is made up of tiny drops of water. Clouds float high in the sky. They are white or gray. **clouds.**

cloud

clown   A **clown** is a person who makes people laugh. **Clowns** wear funny clothes and paint their faces. They do tricks and act silly. **clowns.**

clown

clue   A **clue** helps you answer a question. **Clues** helped John find the answer to the riddle. **clues.**

coal   **Coal** is found under the ground. It is black. **Coal** gives off heat when it is burned.

coat

coat   A **coat** is a piece of clothing worn over other clothes. Grace bought a new winter **coat. coats.**

cold   **1. Cold** means not hot. Winter weather can be **cold. colder, coldest.**
2. Cold also means a kind of sickness. You cough and sneeze when you have a **cold.** Many people get **colds** in the winter. **colds.**

cold

C c

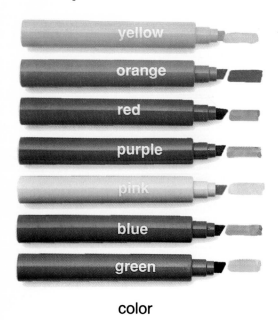

color

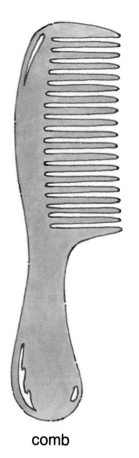

comb

color 1. Red, yellow, blue, green, orange, pink, and purple are **colors**. What **color** is Jane's new jacket? **colors.** 2. **Color** also means to paint or mark with a color. Use a crayon to **color** the sky blue. **colored, coloring.**

colt

colt A **colt** is a young horse or donkey. **colts.**

comb A **comb** is used to keep hair neat. **combs.**

come Can you **come** to my birthday party? My dad will **come** at 6 o'clock. **came, come, coming.**

complete 1. When something is **complete**, no parts are missing. Jim collected a **complete** set of baseball cards. 2. **Complete** also means to get to the end of something. She **completed** her drawing at home. **completed, completing.**

computation   When you find something out by using mathematics, you make a **computation**. Adding 6 and 3 to get 9 is a **computation**. **computations.**

$6+3=9$

computation

computer   A **computer** is a machine that can keep and give back information. A **computer** can do many kinds of work. **Computers** play games and give answers to problems. **computers.**

computer

continent   A **continent** is a very large area of land. There are seven **continents** on the earth. We live on the **continent** of North America. **continents.**

cook

continent

cook   Cook means to make food ready to eat. Food **cooks** on a hot stove. John **cooked** the potatoes. **cooked, cooking.**

C|c

cookie

cookie A **cookie** is a small, flat cake. Kate likes to bake **cookies. cookies.**

cool **Cool** means more cold than hot. The fall day was very **cool. cooler, coolest.**

copy **I.** A **copy** is a thing made to be just like another. Make a **copy** of this page. **copies.**
2. **Copy** also means to make something like something else. **Copy** this picture. **copied, copying.**

corn

corn **Corn** is a yellow or white vegetable. It grows on a tall, green plant. Animals and people eat **corn.**

corner A **corner** is the place where two lines or two sides meet. There was a chair in the **corner** of the room. **corners.**

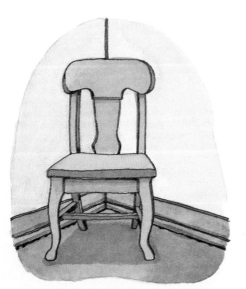

corner

correct
1. **Correct** means right or true. Tom had the **correct** answer.
2. **Correct** also means to check whether something is right or true. The teacher **corrected** my paper. **corrected, correcting.**

THAT'S RIGHT!

NEY OF ... ITH A SINGL

correct

cost
The amount of money needed to buy something is its **cost**. The **cost** of this record is 8 dollars. **costs.**

FOLK MUSIC Special $8.00

cost

cough

cough
Cough means to push air out of the chest with a loud noise. She had a cold and **coughed** all night. **coughed, coughing.**

could
Her brother said he **could** come. When grandpa was young, he **could** dance well.

couldn't
Couldn't means could not. Her sister **couldn't** come.

C | c

count

count   **1.** **Count** means to name numbers in order. She can **count** to 20.
2. **Count** also means to add up. He **counted** the marbles and found there were 12. **counted, counting.**

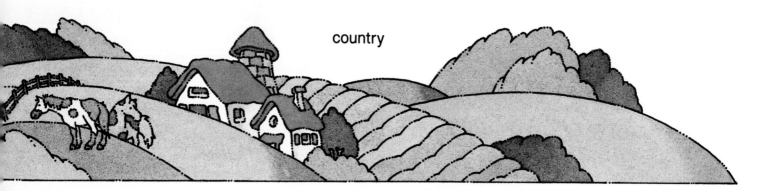

country

country   **1.** The **country** is the land outside a city. There are many farms in the **country.**
2. **Country** also means a land and people with the same leaders. The people of a **country** usually speak the same language. There are many **countries** in the world. Our **country** is the United States. **countries.**

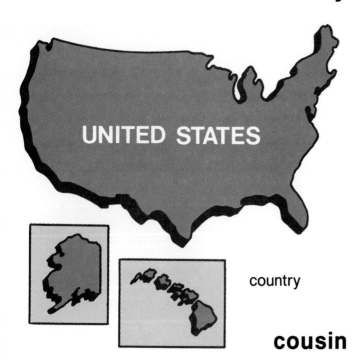

UNITED STATES

country

cousin   Your **cousin** is the son or daughter of any of your uncles or aunts. **cousins.**

cover   When you **cover** something, you put something else over it. **Cover** the baby with a blanket. **covered, covering.**

cover

cow   A **cow** is a large animal. **Cows** eat grass. We get milk from **cows**. **cows.**

cow

crayon   A **crayon** is used for drawing and coloring pictures. **Crayons** come in many colors. **crayons.**

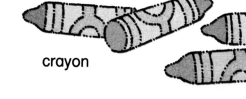

crayon

creep   **Creep** means to move slowly with the body close to the floor. The cat was **creeping** toward the mouse. **crept, creeping.**

C|c

crept

crept The cat **crept** without making a sound.

crib A **crib** is a small bed with high sides. Babies sleep in **cribs. cribs.**

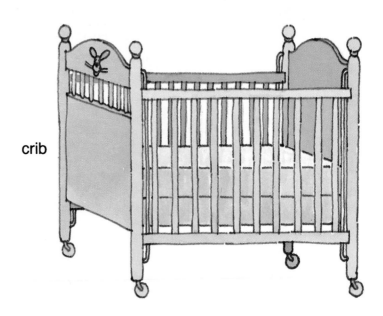

crib

crop Plants grown by farmers for food are **crops**. Corn is an important crop. **crops.**

cross Cross means to move from one side to another. Let's **cross** the street. **crossed, crossing.**

crow

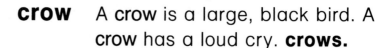

crow A **crow** is a large, black bird. A **crow** has a loud cry. **crows.**

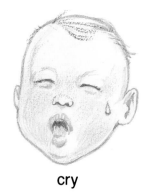

cry　**1.** Cry means to call loudly. He cried, ''Look out!''
2. Cry also means to have tears come from the eyes. Babies **cry** when they are hungry. **cried, crying.**

cry

cup　A **cup** is a dish to drink from. **Cups** are round and deep. You can drink milk from a **cup. cups.**

cup

curtain　A **curtain** is a cloth hung at a window or door. Close the **curtains,** please. **curtains.**

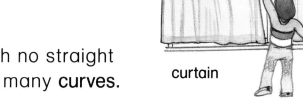

curtain

curve　A **curve** is a line with no straight part. This road has many **curves. curves.**

cut　When you **cut** something, you divide it into pieces. Dad cut the meat with a knife. Juan used scissors to **cut** the paper. **cut, cutting.**

cut

Dd

dad Dad is a short name for father.
dads.

dad

daisy A **daisy** is a flower with a yellow center. **Daisies** have white, pink, or yellow petals. **daisies.**

daisy

dance

dance When you **dance**, you move to the sound of music. We **danced** at the party. **danced, dancing.**

dark When something is not light, it is **dark**. It was so **dark** I could not see. His hair is **dark**. She wore a **dark** blue sweater. **darker, darkest.**

dark

date The **date** of something is the time it happens or happened. May 4, 1982, is her birth **date**. What is the date today? **dates.**

daughter A **daughter** is a girl child. A girl is the **daughter** of her father and mother. The Smiths have four daughters. **daughters.**

daughter

67

D d

day **1.** Day is the time when the sun is up. **Days** are brighter and warmer than nights.

2. A **day** is also 24 hours of light and dark. There are 7 **days** in a week. **days.**

dead

dead When something is **dead**, it is no longer alive. No one watered the flowers, and now they are **dead**.

decide **Decide** means to choose or to make up your mind. Kim **decided** to eat the apple, not the cookie. **decided, deciding.**

deep Something that is **deep** goes a long way down. I dug a **deep** hole. **deeper, deepest.**

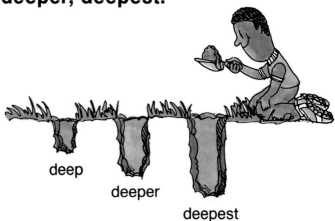
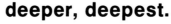
deep deeper deepest

deer A **deer** is an animal that can run very fast. **deer.**

deer

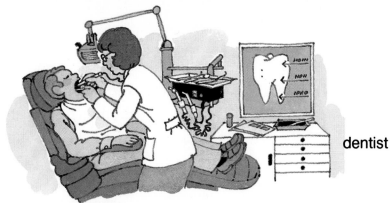

dentist

dentist A **dentist** is a doctor who takes care of people's teeth. **dentists.**

describe To **describe** something is to tell about it. Kate **described** her dog so well, we could almost see it. **described, describing.**

desert

desert A **desert** is a place without water or trees. **Deserts** are usually hot and sandy. **deserts.**

desk A **desk** is where we sit in a classroom. We read and write at our desks. **desks.**

desk

dictionary A **dictionary** is a book that tells what words mean. People also use **dictionaries** to find out how to spell words. **dictionaries.**

did Lee **did** a good job taking care of his dog. **Did** you see Carlos today?

D | d

different

different Different means not alike. These hats are **different**, but these shoes are alike.

dig

dig Dig means to make a hole in the ground. The dog **dug** a place to hide its bone. **dug, digging.**

dime

dime A **dime** is a kind of money equal to ten cents. Ten **dimes** make one dollar. **dimes.**

dining room A dining room is a room in a house where meals are eaten. **dining rooms.**

dining room

dinner Dinner is a meal eaten in the evening. We had chicken for **dinner** last night. **dinners.**

70

dinosaur A **dinosaur** is an animal that lived many years ago. **Dinosaurs** lived on the earth before there were people. Some **dinosaurs** were much bigger than elephants. Some were smaller than cats. **dinosaurs.**

dinosaur

dip **Dip** means to put something in a liquid and quickly take it out again. She **dipped** her toe into the cold lake. **dipped, dipping.**

NORTH

WEST   EAST

SOUTH

direction

direction The **direction** of something is the way it is moving or pointing. In what **direction** are you going? North, south, east, and west are directions. **directions.**

directions **Directions** tell you what to do or how to do something. If you follow the **directions**, you can make this toy.

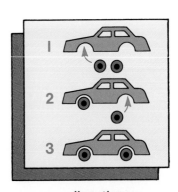

directions

71

D | d

dirt Dirt is something that is not clean. **Dirt** makes other things unclean. The children got **dirt** on their clothes when they played outside.

dirty

dirtier

dirtiest

dirty When something is **dirty**, it is not clean. The children's boots were very **dirty**. **dirtier, dirtiest.**

dish A **dish** is something food is placed on. We eat our meals from **dishes**. **dishes.**

dish

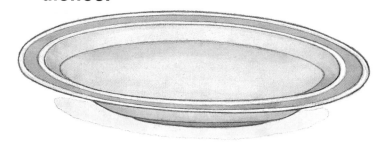

distance The **distance** between two points is the amount of space between them. What is the **distance** between New York and Chicago?

divide

divide When you **divide** something, you break it into equal parts. Lee **divided** the apple into four parts. **divided, dividing.**

do   Do you like peanuts? I **do**! I will **do** my work tomorrow. **does, did, done, doing.**

doctor   A **doctor** is a person who helps sick people. The **doctor** gave me medicine for my cough. **doctors.**

doctor

does   **Does** she like peanuts? Yes, she **does**! He **does** all his work.

dog   A **dog** is an animal. Some **dogs** are big and some are small. Many people keep **dogs** as pets. **dogs.**

dog

doghouse

doghouse   A **doghouse** is a small house for a dog. When it rains or snows, dogs go into their **doghouses**. **doghouses.**

D d

doll

donkey

door

doll A **doll** is a toy that looks like a person. **Dolls** come in many shapes and sizes. **dolls.**

dollar

dollar A **dollar** is a piece of paper money. It is equal to 100 cents. **dollars.**

done She has **done** all her work. Have you **done** all your work?

donkey A **donkey** is an animal with long ears. It looks like a little horse. **donkeys.**

don't **Don't** means do not. **Don't** forget your books. I **don't** want to go out in the rain.

door You open a **door** to go into a building or room. Cars also have **doors.** Some **doors** can be locked. **doors.**

dot

dot A **dot** is a tiny, round mark. Put a **dot** over each ''i'' you write. My new shorts have red **dots** on them. **dots.**

dove A **dove** is a large bird with short legs. **doves.**

dove

down When something goes **down**, it goes from a higher place to a lower place. The pony ran **down** the hill. I sat **down**.

dragon

dragon A **dragon** is a large animal that breathes fire. **Dragons** are make-believe animals. Many old stories tell about **dragons**. They can fly and often fight with people. **dragons.**

drank Pat **drank** four glasses of milk.

D | d

D | d

draw

draw When you **draw**, you make a picture. You can **draw** with pencils, crayons, chalk, or pens. **drew, drawn, drawing.**

drawn I have **drawn** a picture of my cat.

dream A **dream** is something that seems to happen while you sleep. **Dreams** can be good or bad. Bob had a **dream** about playing baseball. **dreams.**

dream

dress

dress **I.** A **dress** is something a girl or woman wears. **Dresses** are a kind of clothing. **dresses.**
2. When you **dress**, you put on your clothes. May is **dressing** for school. **dressed, dressing.**

drew She **drew** a pretty picture.

drink   Drink means to swallow water, milk, or some other liquid. I **drank** a glass of milk. **drank, drunk, drinking.**

drink

drive   Drive means to make a car go. My brother can **drive.** He is **driving** me to school today. **drove, driven, driving.**

driven   He has **driven** me home many times.

driver

driver   A person who drives a car is a driver. **drivers.**

drop

drop   Drop means to let something fall. Chris **dropped** some of the plates. **dropped, dropping.**

drove   My mother **drove** me to school.

D | d

drum

drum   A **drum** makes a sound when it is hit. **Drums** are often hit with sticks. **drums.**

drunk   I have **drunk** four glasses of milk today.

dry

dry   When something has no water in it, it is **dry**. Kate's hair is **dry**, but Lee's is wet. **drier, driest.**

duck   A **duck** is a bird with short legs. **Ducks** live near lakes and rivers. They like to swim. **ducks.**

duck

dug   My dog **dug** a hole in the yard.

dump   **Dump** means to throw down. The girls **dumped** all their toys on the floor. **dumped, dumping.**

dug

Ee

each   Each child gets a balloon.

eagle   An **eagle** is a large bird with long wings. **Eagles** can see things from a great distance. **eagles.**

eagle

E e

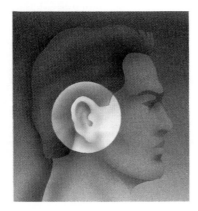

ear

ear   The **ear** is the part of the body that helps you hear. Your **ears** are on each side of your head. **ears.**

early   Early means before the usual time. Let's get up **early** in the morning to take a walk. **earlier, earliest.**

earth

earth   The **earth** is the whole world. All the people and animals live on the **earth**.

east   East is a direction. The sun comes up in the **east**. **East** is the opposite direction to west.

east

easy   Easy means not hard to do or understand. That was an **easy** question to answer. **easier, easiest.**

eat **1.** Eat means to chew and swallow food. Cows **eat** grass.
2. Eat also means to have a meal. Let's **eat**. We will **eat** at Amy's house. **ate, eaten, eating.**

eat

eaten Bob has **eaten** dinner already.

edge Edge means the place where something ends. Her glass was too close to the **edge** of the table. **edges.**

edge

effect An **effect** is what happens because of something else. One **effect** of the heavy rain was water in the streets. **effects.**

egg

egg An **egg** is a food. **Eggs** are laid by chickens and are often eaten at breakfast. Other animals also lay eggs. **eggs.**

elbow The part of the arm that can bend is the **elbow**. **elbows.**

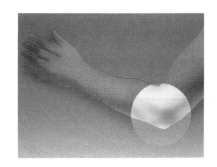

elbow

E|e

electricity

Electricity is a kind of energy that makes light and heat. **Electricity** makes televisions, radios, and other machines work.

electric light

electric light

An **electric light** is a light that works by electricity. We use **electric lights** after it gets dark. **electric lights.**

elephant

An **elephant** is the largest four-footed animal. It has large ears and a long trunk. **elephants.**

elephant

elevator

elevator

An **elevator** is like a small room that moves up and down. **Elevators** carry people up and down in buildings. **elevators.**

elf

An **elf** is a tiny make-believe person in a story. **Elves** are full of tricks. **elves.**

elf

else   Will someone **else** go in my place?
Let's go somewhere **else** for lunch.

elves   Fairy tales often tell about **elves.**

empty   When something is **empty**,
there is nothing in it. The
glass is **empty.**

empty

elves

end   **End** means the last part of
something. Don is at the **end** of the
line. Did you read the **end** of the
story? **ends.**

end

energy   **Energy** makes people and things
able to work and move. People get
energy from food. Electricity is a
form of **energy.**

enough   There is **enough** food for everyone.
Have you eaten **enough?**

E | e

equal

equal 1. Equal means the same. The two dogs are **equal** in size.
2. Equal also means to be the same as something else. Five pennies **equal** one nickel. **equaled, equaling.**

even

estimate Estimate means to make a guess. She **estimated** it would take one hour to do the work. **estimated, estimating.**

even 1. Even means flat and smooth. The ground here is **even**.
2. Even also means at the same height. The snow is **even** with the window.

evening Evening is the time between sunset and going to bed. It gets dark in the evening. **evenings.**

ever Do you **ever** go swimming?

evening

every   Every child loves to play. Read **every** word.

everyone   **Everyone** must bring a book to class.

exercise

exercise   **1.** Exercise means to move the body to improve health. You **exercise** when you run, swim, or play ball. The runner **exercises** every day. **exercised, exercising.** **2.** An **exercise** is something that gives practice. Read the page and then do the **exercise. exercises.**

explain   Explain means to tell about something so people are able to understand. She will **explain** how to play the game. **explained, explaining.**

eye   The **eye** is the part of the body that helps you see. Your eyes are in your face. **Eyes** can be brown, blue, green, gray, and some other colors. **eyes.**

eye

Ff

fable   A **fable** is a story that teaches a lesson. Many **fables** are about talking animals. **fables.**

fable

face   The front part of the head is the **face.** Your eyes, nose, and mouth are part of your **face.** Everyone's **face** is different. **faces.**

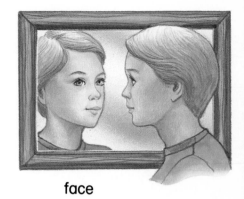

face

fact   A **fact** is something that is known to be true. It is a **fact** that Thanksgiving is a holiday. **facts.**

factory   People make things at a **factory.** TV sets are made in **factories. factories.**

factory

fair¹   Fair means going by the rules. If you are not **fair,** no one will want to play with you. **fairer, fairest.**

fair²

fair²   A **fair** is an outdoor show that is fun to see. **Fairs** have farm animals and other things. They often have rides and games. **fairs.**

F f

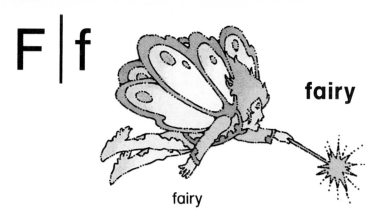

fairy

fairy In stories, a **fairy** is a tiny, make-believe person. **Fairies** can do unusual things. **fairies.**

fall

fallen

fall 1. **Fall** means to drop down from a higher place. She **fell** off the branch of the tree. **fell, fallen, falling.**
2. **Fall** is one of the four seasons. It comes after summer and before winter. The trees lose their leaves in the **fall.** Another name for **fall** is autumn.

fallen The leaves have **fallen** from the tree.

family A mother, a father, and their children make up a **family. Family** also means cousins, aunts, uncles, and grandparents. **families.**

family

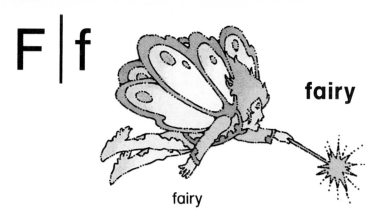

fan

fan A **fan** is a machine that blows the air around. **Fans** keep people cool in hot weather. **fans.**

far   Far means a long way. Our house is far from the ocean. **farther, farthest.**

farm   A farm is the land on which a farmer grows food and raises animals. **farms.**

farm

farmer

farmer   A farmer is a person who works on a farm. Some **farmers** grow corn. Some **farmers** raise chickens. **farmers.**

farther

farther   I jumped **farther** than you did.

farthest   Beth jumped the **farthest** of all.

farthest

fast   **1.** Fast means quick. She is a fast runner.
2. When you go **fast**, you go in a quick way. Some boats go very fast. **faster, fastest.**

fast

Arneson

F|f

fat   Fat means weighing more than usual. That **fat** dog needs exercise. **fatter, fattest.**

fat

father

father   A **father** is a man who has a child or children. **Fathers** and mothers are parents. **fathers.**

favorite   Your **favorite** sport is the sport you like best. Swimming is Jack's **favorite** sport.

feather

feather   A **feather** is part of a bird's body. **Feathers** are soft and light. **feathers.**

fed   Susan **fed** the baby.

feed   **Feed** means to give food to someone. It's time to **feed** the baby. Adam **fed** the dog. **fed, feeding.**

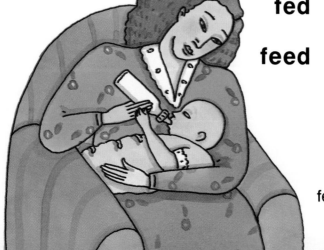

feed

feel

feel **1.** **Feel** means to touch something. Sam likes to **feel** the soft fur of his cat.
2. When you **feel** sad, you are sad in your mind. When you **feel** happy you are happy in your mind. **felt, feeling.**

feeling

feeling A **feeling** is the way you feel about something in your mind. Sadness and love are **feelings.** **feelings.**

feet People have two **feet**, but dogs have four **feet**.

feet

fell The child **fell** off the bicycle.

fell

felt Susan **felt** the mud between her toes.

F | f

91

F f

fence A **fence** around a garden or yard keeps animals out. A **fence** also shows where someone's yard ends. **fences.**

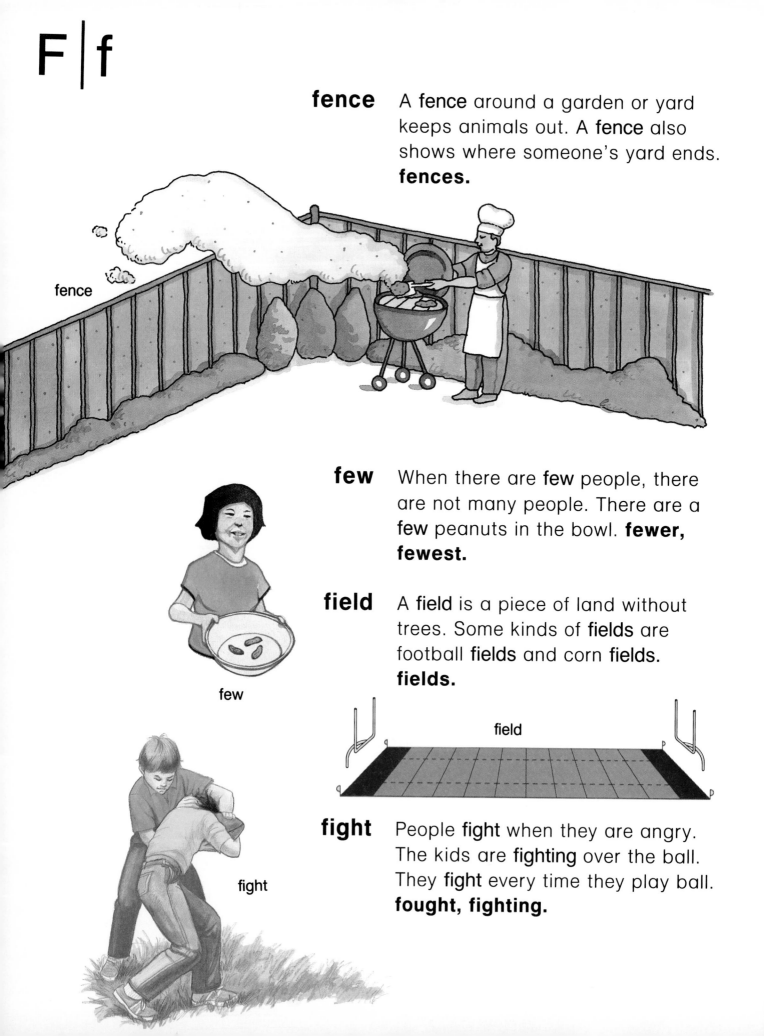

fence

few When there are **few** people, there are not many people. There are a few peanuts in the bowl. **fewer, fewest.**

few

field A **field** is a piece of land without trees. Some kinds of **fields** are football **fields** and corn **fields**. **fields.**

field

fight People **fight** when they are angry. The kids are **fighting** over the ball. They **fight** every time they play ball. **fought, fighting.**

fight

fill Fill means to make something so full that there is no more room. Mr. Jones is **filling** a glass with fruit juice. Jenny **filled** the bowl with apples. **filled, filling.**

fill

find Find means to come upon something. Danny **finds** lots of shells. Did you **find** my gloves? **found, finding.**

find

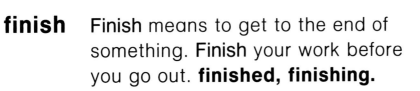

fine Fine means very good. He painted a **fine** picture. It was a **fine** day. **finer, finest.**

finger A finger is a part of the hand. Each hand has five **fingers**. You can pick up things with your fingers. **fingers.**

finger

finish Finish means to get to the end of something. **Finish** your work before you go out. **finished, finishing.**

fire

fire When something burns, it causes a **fire**. **Fires** are hot and can cause harm. Water can put out most **fires**. **fires.**

F | f

firefighter   A **firefighter** is a person whose work is putting out fires. **Firefighters** ride on fire trucks. **firefighters.**

firefighter

first

first   **First** means coming before all others. The **first** letter of the alphabet is A. Ann sang **first.**

fish   A **fish** is an animal that lives in the water. There are many kinds of **fish.** Some kinds live in the ocean. Some live in lakes and rivers. **fish.**

fish

fit

fit   **1.** **Fit** means healthy and strong. Exercise will help to keep your body fit. **fitter, fittest.**
2. **Fit** also means to have the right size or shape. Do the shoes **fit**? **fitted, fitting.**

fix

fix   When you **fix** something broken, you make it work again. Dad and I **fixed** my bicycle. **fixed, fixing.**

flag A **flag** is a piece of colored cloth with stars or other shapes on it. Every country has its own **flag**. The **flag** of the United States is red, white, and blue. **flags.**

flag

flashlight A **flashlight** is a small light you can carry. It helps you see in the dark. **flashlights.**

flashlight

flat Flat means smooth and even. A table has a **flat** top. A football field should be **flat**. **flatter, flattest.**

flew The eagle **flew** over the hill.

float Float means to move slowly on top of the water or in the air. It's fun to **float** in a pool. The red balloon **floated** in the sky. **floated, floating.**

float

F | f

floor

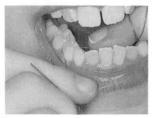
floor

1. A **floor** is the part of a room you walk on. He cleaned the **floor** of his room.
2. Floor can also mean one of the stories of a building. Susan lives on the fifth **floor. floors.**

floss

floss

Floss means to use a special thread to clean between the teeth. I **flossed** my teeth last night. **flossed, flossing.**

flow

flow

Flow means to move like water in a stream. The river **flows** past the town. **flowed, flowing.**

flower

flower

A **flower** is a part of a plant. **Flowers** are pretty and come in many colors. Many **flowers** smell nice. Roses and tulips are **flowers. flowers.**

flown

Have you ever **flown** in an airplane?

fly¹   A **fly** is an insect with two wings. There are many kinds of **flies. flies.**

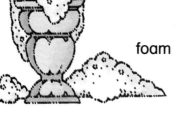
fly¹

fly²   **1.** Fly means to move through the air with wings. Some birds **fly** south for the winter.
2. Fly also means to travel by airplane. We will **fly** to the Rocky Mountains next summer. **flew, flown, flying.**

fly²

foam   Foam is made up of very small bubbles. The **foam** on the soft drink spilled over the top of the glass.

foam

fold

fold   Fold means to bend or turn part of a thing over another part. Please help me **fold** the napkins. **folded, folding.**

folk tale   A folk tale is an old story that has been told for many years by many people. **folk tales.**

follow   Follow means to go after or come after. The dog **followed** me home. Night **follows** day. **followed, following.**

follow

F f

food   Food is what you eat. **Food** helps people grow and gives them energy. Fruit, vegetables, and meats are **food. foods.**

food

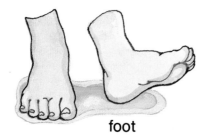

foot

foot   The **foot** is the part of the body at the end of the leg. People walk on their two **feet. feet.**

football   **Football** is a game played on a field. One team tries to kick, throw, or carry the football down the field. The other team tries to stop the first team.

football

for   She went to the store **for** milk. We went **for** a swim. This orange is **for** you.

forest   A **forest** is a place with thick woods. Many animals live in the forest. **forests.**

forest

F | f

forget   Forget means to be unable to remember. Don't **forget** your lunch, Tim. **forgot, forgotten, forgetting.**

forgot   Tim **forgot** to bring his lunch.

forgotten   Tim has **forgotten** his lunch many times.

forget

fork   A **fork** has sharp points and is used to eat with. You lift food from a dish to your mouth with a **fork. forks.**

fork

fought   He **fought** with me today.

found   She **found** a dime on the road.

found

fox

fox   A **fox** is an animal about the size of a small dog. It has a pointed nose and thick fur. **foxes.**

F | f

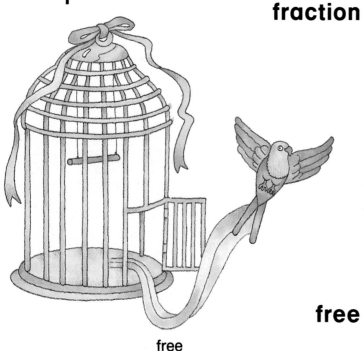

free

fraction   Cut an apple into equal parts. Each part is a **fraction** of the whole thing. Cut a pear into two equal parts. Each part is equal to the fraction 1/2. **fractions.**

fraction

free   **1.** Free means loose, or not shut up. She set the bird **free** from the cage.
2. When something is **free**, you do not have to pay money for it. The show in the park is **free**.

freeze

freeze   When something **freezes**, it becomes very cold and hard. Water turns into ice when it **freezes**. **froze, frozen, freezing.**

fresh   **1.** Fresh means just made or grown. I would like some of that **fresh** bread. **Fresh** tomatoes are good to eat. **fresher, freshest.**
2. When water is **fresh**, it has no salt in it. Rivers and lakes have **fresh** water. People like to drink **fresh** water.

fresh

friend   A **friend** is someone you like and who likes you. It is nice to have friends. **friends.**

friend

frog   A **frog** is a small animal with long back legs. **Frogs** jump from place to place. Most **frogs** live near water. **frogs.**

frog

from   Is Mary home **from** school? Billy took a book **from** the table. Three weeks **from** today is David's birthday.

front   **Front** means the part of anything that faces forward. You see the **front** of our house from the street.

front

froze   It was so cold the pond **froze.**

frozen   Ice is water that has **frozen.**

frozen

fruit   A **fruit** is the part of a tree, bush, or vine that has seeds in it. **Fruit** is good to eat. Apples, oranges, grapes, and strawberries are different kinds of **fruit.**

fruit

F f

full

fry   Fry means to cook in hot fat. He loves to eat **fried** chicken for dinner. **fried, frying.**

full   Full means not able to hold more. The bag is **full. fuller, fullest.**

fun

funny

fun   When you have **fun,** you have a good time. The children had **fun** on the swing.

funny   When something is **funny,** it makes you laugh. The children laughed at the **funny** clown. **funnier, funniest.**

fur

fur   Fur is hair that is thick and soft. It covers the skin of many animals. Some bears have white **fur.**

G g

game   A game is something you can play.
Children like to play **games.**
games.

game

G | g

garage

garage A garage is a place where cars are parked or fixed. Mechanics fix cars in **garages**. My father parks his car in the garage. **garages.**

garden A garden is a place where vegetables or flowers are grown. There are roses in our **garden**. **gardens.**

garden

gas 1. A gas is something that is not liquid or solid. A **gas** has no special size or shape. Air is made up of **gases**. Most **gases** have no color and cannot be seen. **gases.**
2. Gas also means a liquid that is put into cars and other machines to make them go. Our car stopped because it was out of **gas**.

gas

gate A gate is a door in a fence or wall. Be sure to close the gate. **gates.**

gate

gave   Bob **gave** his mother a flower.

geese   **Geese** means more than one goose. The **geese** swam on the lake.

geese

germ   A **germ** is a very tiny animal or plant. **Germs** can be seen only with a microscope. Some **germs** cause people to get sick. **germs.**

get   Sam hopes to **get** presents on his birthday. When I **get** home, I eat a snack. Mom **gets** up early. **got, gotten, getting.**

ghost   In stories, a **ghost** is a white shape that scares people. **Ghosts** are not real. **ghosts.**

ghost

giant

giant   In stories, a **giant** is a person of very large size. **Giants** are very strong. **giants.**

105

G | g

giraffe

give

glad

giraffe   A giraffe is a very tall animal. It has spots on its skin, and has a very long neck. **giraffes.**

girl   A girl grows up to be a woman. The **girls** were playing baseball. **girls.**

give   Give means to hand over something. Mother is **giving** me a birthday present. Give me that pencil. **gave, given, giving.**

given   Were you **given** a glass of juice?

glad   Glad means happy. We were **glad** to see Dad. **gladder, gladdest.**

glass 1. Glass is used for windows and many other things. You can see through **glass**. It is hard, but easy to break.
2. A **glass** is something to drink from. You can drink water or milk from a **glass**. **glasses.**

glass

globe A **globe** is a small copy of the earth. A **globe** is round and has a map of the earth drawn on it. Can you find the United States on the globe? **globes.**

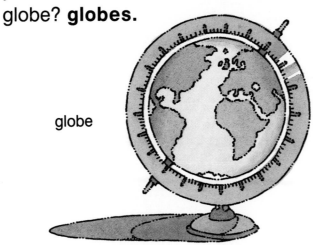
globe

glossary A **glossary** is a list of hard words with their meanings. There is a **glossary** at the end of the book. **glossaries.**

glove

glove A **glove** covers your hand. Gloves keep your hands warm. **gloves.**

glue Glue is something used to stick things together. He used **glue** to fix the broken toy.

glue

G g

go Go means to move from one place to another. Roger likes to **go** to the store. He **goes** there every day. That car is **going** fast. **went, gone, going.**

goat

goat A **goat** is an animal with horns. **Goats** have hair under their chins. **goats.**

goldfish

goldfish A **goldfish** is a small, orange fish. Many people keep **goldfish** in glass bowls. **goldfish.**

gone They have **gone** to a movie.

good When something is **good**, it is right and as it ought to be. If something is **good**, it is not bad. Dad said my drawing was **good**. Rover is a **good** dog. That was a **good** story. **better, best.**

good   better   best

good-by Good-by is something people say when they are going away. People also say **good-by** when they finish talking on the telephone. Ann said **good-by** as she was leaving. **good-bys.**

good-by

goose

goose A goose is a large bird with a long neck. **Geese** like to swim. **geese.**

gorilla A gorilla is a very large ape. Gorillas have long arms. **gorillas.**

gorilla

got She **got** ice skates for her birthday.

gotten He has **gotten** tired of waiting.

got

G | g

grade   A **grade** is a year of study in school. She is in the first **grade**. **grades.**

grandfather   A **grandfather** is the father of your mother or father. **grandfathers.**

grandma   **Grandma** means grandmother. **grandmas.**

grandfather

grandmother

grandmother   A **grandmother** is the mother of your father or mother. **grandmothers.**

grandpa   **Grandpa** means grandfather. **grandpas.**

grape

grape   A **grape** is a small, round fruit. **Grapes** grow on vines. They may be red, purple, or green. **grapes.**

graph   A **graph** is a line or drawing showing information. You could draw a **graph** to show how your weight has changed over the years. **graphs.**

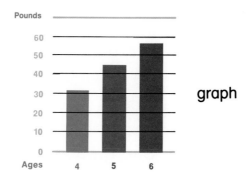

graph

grass   **Grass** is a plant. It is green and grows in fields, parks, and yards. Horses, cows, and sheep eat **grass.**

grass

gray   **Gray** is a color. A hippopotamus is **gray.** Clouds are **gray** before a storm.

great   **1.** **Great** means very big or large. There was a **great** crowd at the picnic.
2. **Great** also means very good. That's a **great** idea you have. **greater, greatest.**

gray

great

G g

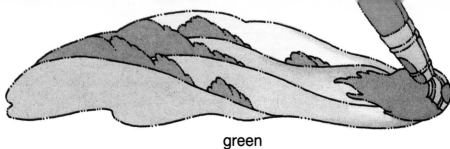

green

greeting

green Green is a color. Grass and leaves are **green** in the summer.

greeting A **greeting** is something you say or do when you meet someone. "Hello" is a **greeting. greetings.**

grew She **grew** two inches this year.

grocery

grocery A **grocery** is a store that sells food. **groceries.**

ground

ground **Ground** means the soil or dirt on the earth. We planted flowers in the **ground.**

group

group A **group** is a number of persons or things together. One **group** of children played ball, and another **group** jumped rope. **groups.**

grow   Grow means to get bigger. Children grow every year. The sunflower is growing fast. **grew, grown, growing.**

grow

grown   The sunflower has **grown** every day.

grown-up   A grown-up is a person who has finished growing. **Grown-ups** are adults. **grown-ups.**

grown-up

guess   Guess means to try to find the answer to something. When you **guess** you are not sure. He **guessed** there would be ten children at the party. **guessed, guessing.**

guitar

guitar   A guitar makes music. You play a **guitar** with your fingers. He played a song on his **guitar**. **guitars.**

Hh

had   Pat **had** a cold. He **had** to stay in bed.

hair   Hair grows on your head. **Hair** can be brown, black, yellow, red, white, or gray. **hairs.**

hair

half   A **half** is one of two equal parts. I cut my apple in **half** and shared it with Eric. Kay ate **half** a sandwich. **halves.**

halves

halves   Halves are more than one half. Two **halves** make a whole.

ham   Ham is meat from a hog. Liz ate a ham sandwich. **hams.**

ham

hamburger   Hamburger is meat from a cow. **Hamburgers** are cooked in a round, flat shape. They are often eaten in a sandwich. **hamburgers.**

hamburger

hammer

hammer   A **hammer** is a tool used for hitting nails. **hammers.**

hamster   A hamster is an animal that looks like a mouse. Some people keep hamsters as pets. **hamsters.**

hamster

115

H | h

hand   **I.** The **hand** is the part of the body at the end of the arm. People can hold things in their **hands**.
2. A **hand** is also part of a clock. Clock **hands** show the hours and the minutes in a day. **hands.**

hand

hang   To **hang** means to be held from above. Kay can **hang** by her knees. Please **hang** up your coat. **hung, hanging.**

hang

happen   Happen means to take place. What happened at the party? **happened, happening.**

happy

happy   When you are **happy**, you feel good about things. Amy was **happy** to see her friend. **happier, happiest.**

hard

hard   **1.** Something that is **hard** is solid, not soft. The red chair is soft, but the wooden chair is **hard**.
2. Hard also means taking a lot of work or energy. When something is **hard** it is not easy. Washing the car was a **hard** job. **harder, hardest.**

harm   **Harm** is something that hurts or causes pain. If you follow the safety rules, you should come to no **harm.**

has

has   Pat still **has** a cold. He **has** to stay in bed. Kate **has** a new dog.

hat

hat   A **hat** is something you wear on your head. **hats.**

have   Pat and I both **have** colds. We **have** to stay in bed. The Burkes **have** a new TV. **has, had, having.**

have

H | h

hay
Hay is special food for horses and cows. It is made up of dried plants and grass.

hay

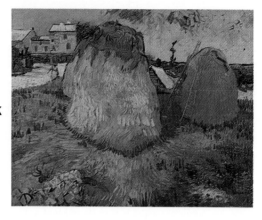

haystack

haystack
A haystack is a large amount of hay stored outside. **haystacks.**

he

he
Who is **he? He** is my friend, Lee. **He** likes to sing.

head

head
The **head** is the top part of your body, above the neck. Your brain, eyes, nose, mouth, and ears are in your **head. heads.**

health
Health means being well, not sick. Good food, sleep, and exercise are important to your **health.**

healthy

healthy
Healthy means to be in good health. Prince is a very **healthy** dog. **healthier, healthiest.**

hear   We **hear** by taking in sounds through our ears. I **hear** a knock at the door. Prince **heard** the sound too. **heard, hearing.**

hear

heard   When Prince **heard** the sound, he began to bark.

heard

hearing   **Hearing** is the sense that lets us take in sounds through our ears. My dog's **hearing** is very good.

heart   The **heart** is a part of the body. Your **heart** is inside your chest. When you run, your **heart** beats fast. **hearts.**

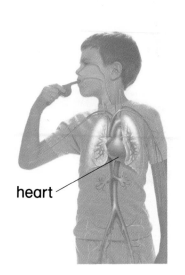

heart

heat   **Heat** means to make something warm or hot. Sue **heated** soup on the stove. **heated, heating.**

heat

H|h

heavy

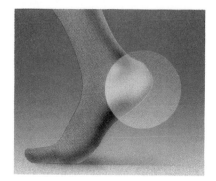

heel

heavy   When something is **heavy**, it weighs very much. An elephant is **heavy**, but a rabbit is light. **heavier, heaviest.**

heel   The **heel** is the back part of the foot. **heels.**

held   The father **held** his baby in his arms.

helicopter

helicopter   A **helicopter** is a machine that flies. **Helicopters** can fly straight up in the air. **helicopters.**

hello   When you meet someone, you say **hello**. Jenny said **hello** to me.

hello   hello!

help   When you **help** someone, you do something useful for them. Tom **helped** his mother wash the car. **helped, helping.**

120

helper   A **helper** is someone who helps others. Tom is a good **helper**. **helpers.**

hen   A **hen** is a chicken that lays eggs. **hens.**

hen

her   I like **her**. I do not like **her** dog. Give **her** the book.

her

here   Please come **here**. **Here** is your present.

hid

hid   The kitten **hid** behind a tree. She **hid** from the big dog.

hidden   The kitten was well **hidden** from the dog.

H | h

high

hide Hide means to try to keep out of sight. My kitten always **hides** from the big dog. **hid, hidden, hiding.**

high When something is **high**, it is up above the ground. The kite is too **high** for Sam to reach. Kate can jump **high**. **higher, highest.**

hill A **hill** is a high piece of ground. **Hills** are smaller than mountains. **hills.**

him

him I like **him**. I gave **him** my apple. When did you give it to **him**?

hippopotamus

his

hippopotamus A **hippopotamus** is a very large animal. **Hippopotamuses** have thick skin without hair. They live near rivers. **hippopotamuses.**

his **His** name is Marco. This is **his** dog. My dog is young, but **his** is old.

caption: hit

hit   Hit means to push hard against something. Jenny **hit** the ball with her bat. Bob **hit** his brother in the arm. **hit, hitting.**

hog

hog   A **hog** is a pig raised for food. **hogs.**

hold   **1.** To **hold** something is to take it in your hands or arms. Please **hold** my coat. Nick **held** the baby.
2. Hold also means to have space for something. This big glass **holds** a lot of water. **held, holding.**

hold

hole   A **hole** is an empty space in something. I dug a **hole** in the ground. There is a **hole** in my sweater. **holes.**

hole

holiday   A **holiday** is a special day. People do not work or go to school on **holidays.** Thanksgiving is a **holiday. holidays.**

H | h

honey

home   Your **home** is the place where you live. Gail's **home** is on Oak Street. **homes.**

honey   Honey is the sweet liquid made by bees. **Honey** tastes good on bread.

hook   A **hook** is something to hang things on. Sam hung his hat on a **hook**. **hooks.**

hook

hop   Hop means to jump. The rabbit **hopped** away. Jane **hops** on one foot. **hopped, hopping.**

hop

hope   Hope means to want something to happen. I **hope** you are well soon. **hoped, hoping.**

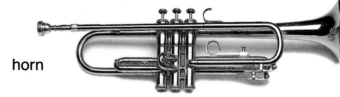

horn

horn   **1.** A **horn** makes music when you blow into it.
2. A **horn** is also a hard, pointed part of an animal's head. Cattle and goats have **horns**. **horns.**

horn

horse   A **horse** is a large animal. **Horses** can run fast. Many people like to ride **horses**. **horses.**

horse

hose   A **hose** is a long tube used to carry water. Lee brought the **hose** to water the flowers. **hoses.**

hospital   A **hospital** is a place where sick people go. The doctors and nurses in the **hospital** help these people. **hospitals.**

hospital

hot   When something is **hot**, it is very, very warm. A sunny day in August can be **hot**. Fire is **hot**. Do not touch the **hot** stove. **hotter, hottest.**

hot

hot dog

hot dog   A **hot dog** is a food made of meat. It has a long, round shape. We ate **hot dogs** on rolls at the picnic. **hot dogs.**

125

H | h

hour

hotel A hotel is a place where people can stay when they are traveling. Hotels have many rooms. **hotels.**

hour An hour is used to measure time. There are 60 minutes in one hour. Twenty-four hours make one day. **hours.**

house A house is a building where people live. Mary's house is in the city. Nick's house is in the country. **houses.**

house

hug

how How is Jim today? How far away do you live? How did this happen?

hug Hug means to hold someone in your arms. Meg hugged her mom. **hugged, hugging.**

hum Hum means to make a singing sound with the lips closed. Kelly hummed as she wrote. **hummed, humming.**

H | h

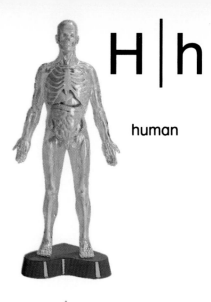

human

human   When something is **human**, it is about people. A **human** body is the body of a person. All people are **human** beings.

hummingbird   A **hummingbird** is a very small bird. **Hummingbirds** have long bills and narrow wings that move very fast. **hummingbirds.**

hummingbird

hung   Sam **hung** his hat on the hook. Jenny **hung** by her knees.

hungry   When you are **hungry**, you feel the need to eat. Kay was so **hungry** she ate a sandwich and a pear. **hungrier, hungriest.**

hungry

hurry   Hurry means to go very quickly. I had to **hurry** because I was late. **hurried, hurrying.**

hurt   Hurt means to be in pain. Mike's foot **hurts**. He **hurt** his foot on a rock. **hurt, hurting.**

OW!

hurt

127

I i

I   I watched television last night.

ice   Ice is frozen water. In winter there is **ice** on the pond. She put two pieces of **ice** in her lemonade.

ice

ice cream

ice cream   Ice cream is a frozen food. It is sweet. Let's have **ice cream** after dinner.

ice skate

ice skate   An ice skate is a kind of shoe with a piece of metal on the bottom for skating on ice. **ice skates.**

idea

idea   An idea is a thought or plan. It was my **idea** to sell lemonade. **ideas.**

if   You can come if you want to. Let's see **if** Ann wants to come.

iguana

iguana   An iguana is a large lizard that lives in warm places. **Iguanas** like to swim. **iguanas.**

I | i

I'm I'm means I am. I'm going to the circus tomorrow.

imagine

important

imagine Imagine means to make a picture of something in the mind. Can you imagine a world of dinosaurs? **imagined, imagining.**

important **1.** Important means having great meaning. Your birthday is an important day.
2. Important also means well-known. A king is an important person.

in

in The white cat is in the house, and the black cat is out. It is cold here in winter. Be home in time for lunch. Please come in.

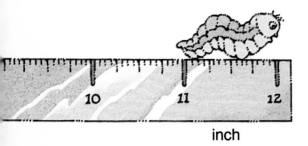

inch

inch An inch is used to measure how long something is. A ruler shows how long an inch is. **inches.**

information   Information means facts that are known. James has a lot of information about dogs.

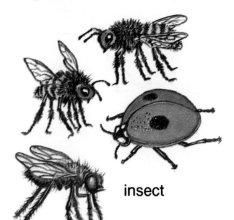

information

insect   An insect is any small animal with six legs. Insects have wings, and their bodies are divided into three parts. Flies and bees are insects. **insects.**

insect

inside   The inside of our house needs painting. There are people inside the store. John stayed inside because it was raining.

inside

into   Come into the house. It was so cold the water turned into ice.

invite   Invite means to ask someone to come to some place or to do something. Gail invited us to her party. **invited, inviting.**

invite

131

I i

iron

iron　Iron means to make clothes smooth. Mother **ironed** four dresses after work. **ironed, ironing.**

is　Her dog **is** outside. **Is** it starting to rain?

island　An **island** is land with water all around it. There are many **islands** in the ocean. **islands.**

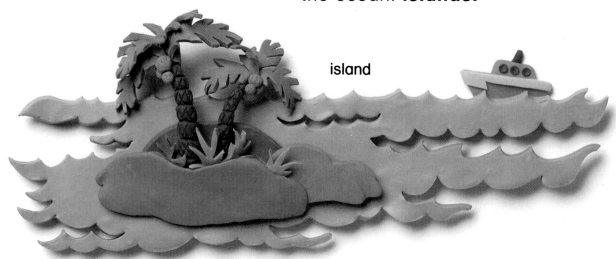

island

it　**It** is nine o'clock in the morning. **Is** it too early to telephone Jack? My ball is at his house and I need **it.**

its　The dog hid **its** bone under my bed.

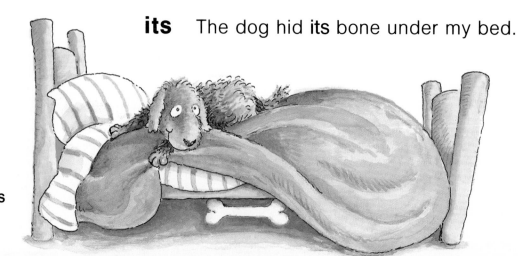

its

joke A joke is something you say or do to make people laugh. Gary told me a funny joke. **jokes.**

"Eat your peas, they'll put color in your cheeks!"

"Who wants green cheeks?"

joke

judge A judge decides who is right and who is wrong. Sometimes judges decide who wins a game. **judges.**

juice Juice is the liquid part of fruits and vegetables. Would you like some orange juice? **juices.**

jump When you **jump,** you push your whole body up or off something. Jane **jumped** and caught the ball. Then she **jumped** off the side of the pool. **jumped, jumping.**

jump rope You use a **jump rope** to play a game. You swing the rope and jump over it. **jump ropes.**

just He is **just** walking around the block. She **just** left a minute ago.

Jj

jacket A jacket is a kind of short coat. Boys and girls wear jackets in cool weather. **jackets.**

jacket

J j

jacks Jacks is a gam[e]
and small, har[d]
are picked up [or]
bounced.

jacks

jar A jar is used to
look like wide b[...]
are made of gl[...]
comes in a **jar**. j[...]

jar

jeans

jeans Jeans are a kin[d]
jeans when you [...]

jelly Jelly is a food m[...]
and sugar. **Jelly**
toast or bread. j[...]

jet A jet is a kind of
flew toward the [...]

job A job is the work[...]
to do. My **job** is [...]
clean. His **job** is [...]

jet

134

K k

kangaroo A kangaroo is an animal with strong back legs. A **kangaroo** can move very fast by jumping. A baby **kangaroo** is carried in a kind of pocket in front of its mother's stomach. **kangaroos.**

kangaroo

136

keep Keep means to have something for a time. Can you **keep** a secret? Joy **keeps** her money in a bank. **Keep** your toys in your room. **kept, keeping.**

keep

kept Dan **kept** his books on the shelf.

key A **key** opens and closes a lock. Dad forgot his **key**, so he couldn't open the car door. **keys.**

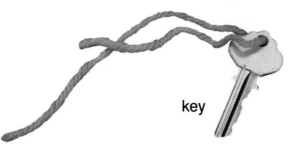

key

kick When you **kick** something, you hit it with your foot. George was **kicking** the ball. He **kicked** it into a tree. **kicked, kicking.**

kick

kid 1. A **kid** is a baby goat.
2. **Kid** also means a child. The **kids** are riding their bikes. **kids.**

kid

kid

K|k

kind²

kind¹   Kind means friendly or nice. The **kind** boy helped Grandma carry the boxes. **kinder, kindest.**

kind²   Kind means a group of things that are alike in some way. Meat is a **kind** of food. Fruit and vegetables are other **kinds** of food. **kinds.**

kindergarten   Kindergarten is the year of school before first grade. **kindergartens.**

king   A king is a man who rules a country and its people. **Kings** have great power. **kings.**

king

kiss

kiss   Kiss means to touch with the lips. Lee's mother **kissed** him as he left. **kissed, kissing.**

kitchen   A kitchen is a room where food is cooked and kept. **Kitchens** have refrigerators and stoves. Many people like to eat in the **kitchen**. **kitchens.**

kitchen

138

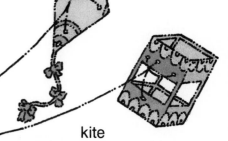

kite A **kite** is a toy that you fly with a string. Most **kites** are made of light wood and paper. We like to fly kites. **kites.**

kite

kitten A **kitten** is a baby cat. **kittens.**

kitten

knee The **knee** is the part of the leg that can bend. You bend your **knees** when you walk or sit. **knees.**

knee

knew He **knew** the answer.

knife A **knife** is used to cut food and other things. **Knives** are sharp. **knives.**

know Know means to have facts about someone or something. Do you **know** how to swim? Julie **knows** everyone in her class. **knew, known, knowing.**

knife

known I have **known** Bob a long time.

L l

ladder   A **ladder** is a set of steps used to climb up and down. Dad used a **ladder** to get to the roof of our house. **ladders.**

ladder

lake   A **lake** is water with land around it. You can sail a boat on a **lake**. **lakes.**

lake

lamb   A **lamb** is a baby sheep. **lambs.**

lamb

lamp   A **lamp** gives light. Jan turned on the **lamp** so she could read. **lamps.**

lamp

land   1. **Land** is the solid part of the earth. People live on the **land**, not the water.
2. **Land** also means ground or soil. The farmer planted corn on his **land**.

language   Language is words, spoken or written. In the United States, most people speak the English **language**. **languages.**

land

141

L | l

lap

lap When you sit down, your upper legs become a **lap**. Sam held his little sister on his **lap. laps.**

large

large If something is **large**, it is big. The children were carrying a **large** box. **larger, largest.**

last[1]

last[1] Last means coming after all others. Danny took the **last** seat in the row.

last[2] Last means to keep on. The snow **lasted** all day. How long did your bad cold **last**? **lasted, lasting.**

late Late means after the usual time. Hurry or you'll be **late** for school. **later, latest.**

laugh Laugh means to make happy sounds when you think something is funny. Lisa **laughed** at the clown. **laughed, laughing.**

late

leader   A **leader** is someone who shows the way or goes first. Ann is the **leader** of the band. **leaders.**

leader

leaf   A **leaf** is part of a tree or plant. A tree or plant has many **leaves** in summer. Most **leaves** are green. **leaves.**

leaf

learn   **Learn** means to find out about something. We **learn** to read and write in school. **learned, learning.**

learn

leave   **1. Leave** means to go away. He leaves school at the same time every day. **2. Leave** also means to go without taking something. **Leave** your books on your desk. **left, leaving.**

leaves   **Leaves** change their colors in the fall.

leaves

L l

left[1]

left[1] Left is the opposite direction from right. Each person has a **left** hand and a right hand. We read words from **left** to right. Turn **left** at the corner.

left[2] She **left** her money at home.

leg The **leg** is a part of the body. People and animals stand and move about on their **legs**. People have two **legs**. Many animals have four legs. **legs.**

leg

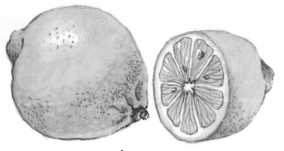

lemon

lemon A **lemon** is a sour, yellow fruit that grows on trees. The juice of **lemons** is used to make lemonade. **lemons.**

length Length means how long something is. The pencil is five inches in **length**. The **length** of the movie was two hours. **lengths.**

length

leopard

leopard A **leopard** is a large animal like a cat. Most **leopards** have spots. **leopards.**

less Two is **less** than four. One piece of candy is **less** than two pieces of candy. There was **less** rain this year than last year.

less

lesson A **lesson** is something you learn or are taught. Molly takes piano lessons. **lessons.**

lesson

let Let means to not stop someone from doing something. I **let** Jane ride my bike. Will your mother **let** you go to the store? **let, letting.**

letter 1. A **letter** is a part of the alphabet. A and B are **letters**. There are twenty-six **letters** in the alphabet. 2. **Letter** also means a written note. Kathy got a **letter** from her mother. **letters.**

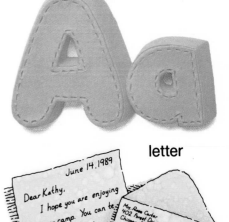
letter

June 14, 1989

Dear Kathy,
I hope you are enjoying summer camp. You can tell me all about it when you get home. I will see you next week. We a...
Have fun.
Love,
Mom

Mrs. Rose Carter
402 Forest Drive
Chicago, IL 60611

Kathy Carter
Camp Hiawatha
Compton, WI 54555

L l

lettuce

lettuce Lettuce is a green vegetable. It is the leaves of a plant. **Lettuce** is used in salads.

librarian

library

librarian A librarian is someone who works in a library. You can ask the **librarian** for help in finding a book. **librarians.**

library A library is a room or building where books are kept. You can take books out at most **libraries. libraries.**

lick

lick Lick means to move the tongue over something. Sue **licked** the ice cream. **licked, licking.**

life **1.** People, animals, and plants have **life.** Having **life** means being alive, breathing, and growing. Rocks do not have **life.**
2. Life also means the time a person, an animal, or a plant is alive. My grandfather had a long **life. lives.**

light¹   **1.** Light comes from the sun. We need **light** to see. We have **light** during the day and darkness at night. **2. Light** also means something, like a lamp or candle, that gives brightness. Turn the **light** on. **lights.**

light¹

light²   When something is **light**, it weighs very little. A rabbit is **light**, but an elephant is heavy. **lighter, lightest.**

light²

lightning   Lightning is a flash of electricity in the sky. **Lightning** struck the tree.

lightning

like¹   Like means the same as. My toy is just **like** yours.

like²   Like means to be pleased with something or someone. Most people **like** apple pie. I **like** all my friends. **liked, liking.**

like¹

147

L l

line

line   A **line** is a long, thin mark. Some **lines** are straight and some are curved. You can draw **lines** on paper. **lines.**

lion   A **lion** is a large animal like a cat. Some **lions** have long hair around their heads. **lions.**

lion

lip

lip   Your mouth has an upper **lip** and a lower **lip.** You blow through your **lips** when you whistle. **lips.**

liquid

liquid   A **liquid** is something that flows freely like water. It is not a solid or a gas. Juice and milk are **liquids. liquids.**

list

list   When you write your favorite toys on a piece of paper, you make a **list.** I made a **list** of things to buy at the store. **lists.**

listen   Listen means to hear or try to hear. Listen to the thunder. We **listened** to the band. **listened, listening.**

listen

little   If something is **little**, it is not big. His pet is a **little** kitten. **littler, littlest.**

little

live¹   **1.** Live means to be alive, to breathe and grow. Animals **live**, but rocks do not.
2. Live also means to make your home in a place. We **live** in a big city. Squirrels **live** in trees. **lived, living.**
Live¹ sounds like give.

 live¹

live²   Live means having life. We saw a real, **live** tiger at the fair. Live² sounds like drive.

lives   They say a cat has nine lives.

L l

living room   A living room is a room in a house or apartment. A living room is used by the whole family. We watch television in the living room. **living rooms.**

living room

lizard

lizard   A lizard is an animal like a snake. It has four legs and a long tail. **lizards.**

lobster   A lobster is an animal that lives in the ocean. Lobsters have hard shells. They are good to eat. **lobsters.**

lobster

lock   A lock is used to keep something closed. Some doors and windows have locks. Many locks must be opened with keys. **locks.**

lock

150

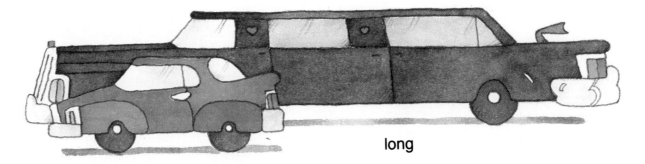

long

long **1.** When something is **long**, it measures a lot from end to end. An inch is short, and a mile is **long**.
2. Long also means lasting for some time. We went on a **long** trip last summer. **longer, longest.**

look

look **1. Look** means to turn the eyes to see something. **Look** at that airplane!
2. Look also means to try to find. He is **looking** for his key. **looked, looking.**

lose **1.** When you **lose** something, you are not able to find it. Be careful not to **lose** your money.
2. Lose also means to not win. Did your team win or lose? **lost, losing.**

lost Luis **lost** his money.

lost

L l

lot

low

lunch

lot A **lot** means a great number or a large amount of something. There were a **lot** of birds on the roof. Ann made **lots** of sandwiches. **lots.**

loud When something is **loud,** it makes a lot of noise. The television is too **loud. louder, loudest.**

love

love 1. Love means a warm, good feeling for someone or something. Liz feels **love** for her puppy.
2. **Love** also means to have a warm, good feeling for someone or something. Jack **loves** all his friends. **loved, loving.**

low Low means near the ground, or not high. There are **low** bushes in front of our house. The wall was so **low** I climbed over it. **lower, lowest.**

lunch Lunch is a meal eaten in the middle of the day. We had sandwiches for lunch today. **lunches.**

M m

machine   A **machine** has moving parts that make it work. **Machines** help people to get things done faster and more easily. Airplanes, washers, and cars are **machines. machines.**

machine

M|m

made

made   Mother **made** lemonade.

magnet   A **magnet** is a piece of metal that pulls other pieces of metal to it. Nails will stick to a **magnet**. **magnets.**

magnet

mail

mail   1. Letters, cards, and packages are **mail**. Mail carriers bring the mail.
2. **Mail** also means to send a letter, card, or package to someone. Rose **mailed** a birthday card to her aunt. **mailed, mailing.**

mailbox A **mailbox** is a place where you mail letters or cards. A **mailbox** is also a place where mail is left for you. **mailboxes.**

mail carrier   mailbox

mail carrier A mail **carrier** is a person whose job is bringing mail to people. **Mail carriers** bring letters and other mail from the post office. **mail carriers.**

make **1.** Make means to put together or build something. Let's **make** a boat. She **made** a cake.
2. Make also means to cause something to take place. Thunder **makes** a loud noise. You **make** me laugh. **made, making.**

make

make-believe Make-believe means not real. Dragons are make-believe animals.

make-believe

mama Mama is another name for mother. **mamas.**

man A boy grows up to be a **man**. Boys grow up to be **men**. **men.**

many How **many** days are there in a week? There are too **many** beans on my plate. I can't eat that **many**.

many

man

155

M|m

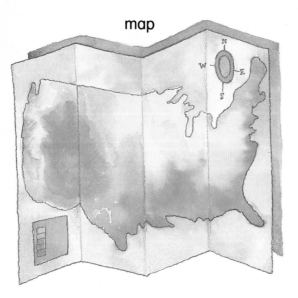
map

map   A **map** is a drawing of an area of the earth that shows many places. **Maps** show countries, cities, rivers, seas, and lakes. **maps.**

marble

marble   A **marble** is a small glass ball used to play games. **Marbles** are usually colored. **marbles.**

mark   A **mark** is a line or dot made on something. Tom made a **mark** on the wall. A period is a **mark** put at the end of a sentence. **marks.**

market   A **market** is a place where people buy and sell things. The farmer took his pigs to the **market**. **markets.**

market

match¹   A **match** is a short stick of wood or paper. The top catches fire when you rub it against some things. **Matches** can be dangerous. **matches.**

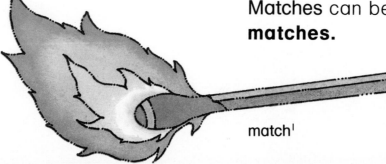
match¹

156

match² Match means to go well together. Her sweater **matches** her socks. Choose the word in the list that **matches** each picture. **matched, matching.**

match²

math Math is a short word for mathematics.

mathematics

mathematics Mathematics is the study of numbers. Adding and subtracting are a part of **mathematics.**

may May we go outside to play? We **may** go to the circus tonight.

maybe Maybe Jan and I will go to the game. **Maybe** our team will win.

me He saw **me** at the swimming pool. The secret is between you and **me.**

meadow A **meadow** is a piece of land where grass grows. **meadows.**

meadow

M | m

meal A **meal** is the food eaten at one time. We eat three **meals** a day. The morning **meal** is breakfast. **meals.**

meal

mean¹ **1.** If you **mean** to do something, you plan to do it. He didn't **mean** to break the window.
2. When you know what something says, you know what it **means.** Cold **means** not hot. What does this word mean? **meant, meaning.**

mean²

mean² Someone who is **mean** is not nice or kind. It is **mean** to hurt someone's feelings. Cinderella's family was **mean** to her. **meaner, meanest.**

meant What do you think she **meant**? He never **meant** to hurt the cat.

measure **Measure** means to find the amount or size of something. The doctor **measured** Jan to see how tall she was. **measured, measuring.**

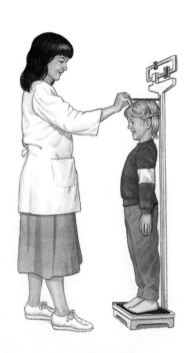
measure

meat　Meat is a kind of food that comes from animals. Hamburger and ham are kinds of **meat**.

meat

mechanic　A mechanic is a person whose job is fixing machines. Some **mechanics** work in garages. **mechanics.**

mechanic

medicine　Medicine is something used to make a sick person well. Doctors tell sick people what **medicine** to take. Remember to take the **medicine** for your cold. **medicines.**

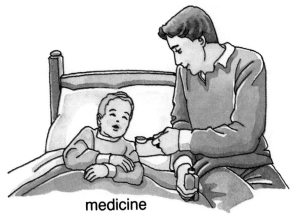
medicine

meet　Meet means to come together. Would you like to **meet** Mister Rogers? **Meet** me in front of the playground. **met, meeting.**

meet

men　Boys grow up to be **men**.

met　We **met** our friends at the park.

M m

mice   Mice means more than one mouse. We saw field **mice** in the yard.

mice

microscope   A **microscope** is used to make things look bigger. A **microscope** helps you see things that are too small to see with your eyes. **microscopes.**

microscope

microwave   A **microwave** is a special kind of oven. **Microwaves** cook food very quickly. **microwaves.**

microwave

middle   The **middle** of something is its center. The soccer ball is in the **middle** of the field.

middle

might   We **might** go ice skating if it stays cold.

milk Milk is a drink that comes from cows. It is white. Drinking **milk** every day helps you grow.

milk

mind The **mind** is the part of a person that thinks and feels. You use your **mind** to learn and to imagine. **minds.**

mine That bike is **mine.**

mine

minute A **minute** is a short period of time. Sixty seconds equal one **minute.** Sixty **minutes** equal one hour. **minutes.**

minute

miss **1.** To **miss** something means not to get it. Lucy tried to catch the ball, but **missed** it. She **missed** her bus. **2. Miss** also means to feel bad because someone is gone. Maria **missed** her family when she was away at camp. **missed, missing.**

miss

M|m

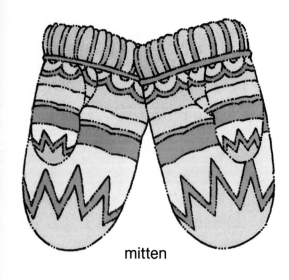

mitten

Miss   Miss is used before the name of a woman who is not married. A young girl is sometimes called Miss. **Misses.**

mitten   A mitten covers the hand. It has a special place for the thumb. Mittens keep your hands warm when it is cold outside. **mittens.**

mix

mom

mix   Mix means to put together. You mix eggs, sugar, chocolate, and other things to make these cookies. **mixed, mixing.**

mom   Mom is another name for mother. **moms.**

money   Pennies, nickels, dimes, and dollars are **money**. People buy things with **money**. People who work at jobs are paid **money**.

money

monkey A monkey is an animal with long arms and legs. There are many different kinds of monkeys. Some monkeys live in trees. **monkeys.**

monkey

monster A monster is a make-believe person or animal. Monsters are big or scary. In stories, some monsters are friendly and some are not. Dragons are monsters. **monsters.**

monster

month A month is a part of a year. There are twelve months in a year. They are January, February, March, April, May, June, July, August, September, October, November, and December. **months.**

moon

moon The moon is the biggest and brightest thing in the sky at night. The moon goes around the earth.

M | m

mop

mop   You use a **mop** to clean the floor. A mop has a long handle. **mops.**

more   A dime is **more** than a penny. I would like **more** soup. This picture is **more** beautiful than that one.

morning   Morning is the early part of the day. **Morning** ends at noon. **mornings.**

morning

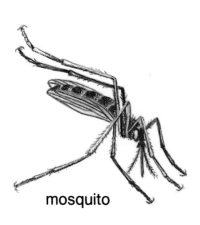
mosquito

mosquito   A **mosquito** is an insect that flies. Some **mosquitoes** bite people. **mosquitoes.**

most   Sam did the **most** work. **Most** people like pizza. The **most** beautiful kitten is the black one.

mother   A **mother** is a woman who has a child or children. **Mothers** and fathers are parents. **mothers.**

mother

164

motor   A **motor** is a kind of machine that makes other machines work. **Motors** run on electricity or gas. Cars have **motors** that make them move. **motors.**

motor

mountain   A **mountain** is a very high hill. Some **mountains** have snow on top. **mountains.**

mountain

mouse   A **mouse** is a small animal with a long tail. Some **mice** live in people's houses. Some **mice** live in fields and meadows. **mice.**

mouse

mouth   The **mouth** is the part of the body that helps you eat and talk. It is part of the face. Your teeth and tongue are in your **mouth**. **mouths.**

mouth

M | m

move

move Move means to go from one place to another. May I **move** to a different desk? Her family **moved** to a new house. **moved, moving.**

movie A **movie** tells a story with pictures. Bob loves to watch **movies**. **movies.**

movie

Mr.   Mrs.   Ms.
         or   or
         Ms.   Miss

Mr. Mr. is used before a man's name.

Mrs. Mrs. is used before a married woman's name.

Ms. Ms. is used before a woman's name.

much How **much** time do we have for swimming? I like swimming very **much.**

muscle A **muscle** is a part of the body that helps you move. Without **muscles**, you could not lift or carry things. There are over 600 **muscles** in your body. **muscles.**

muscle

music The sounds made by a piano, a violin, a guitar, and other instruments are **music**. The sound of a person singing is **music**. People like to listen to **music**.

music

must I would like to stay, but I **must** leave. I **must** go home for dinner now.

my I lost **my** mittens in the park. I was playing with **my** friends.

myself I saw **myself** in the mirror.

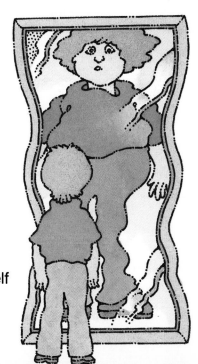
myself

167

Nn

nail **1.** A **nail** is a thin piece of metal with a point at one end. **Nails** hold pieces of wood together.
2. Nail also means the hard part at the end of a finger or toe. **nails.**

nail

name   Your **name** is what people call you. Everyone has a **name**. Countries and cities also have **names**. The players' **names** are on their shirts. **names.**

name

nap   A **nap** is a short sleep. Do you take an afternoon nap? **naps.**

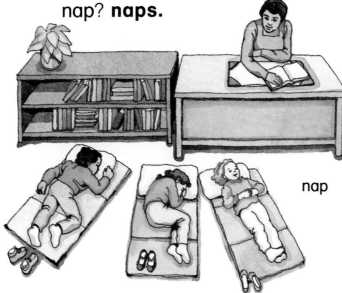

nap

napkin   A **napkin** is a piece of cloth or paper. **Napkins** are used at meals to protect clothes and to clean the lips and fingers. **napkins.**

napkin

nature   **Nature** means everything not made by people. Plants, animals, air, water, and people are part of **nature**. The earth and its mountains, oceans, and rivers are part of **nature**.

N | n

neck

near Her birthday is **near**. We are **near** the toy store. **nearer, nearest.**

neck The **neck** is the part of the body between the head and shoulders. **necks.**

necklace

necklace A **necklace** is something worn around the neck. Mom wore a beautiful **necklace** at the party. **necklaces.**

need

need When you **need** something, you must have it. The hungry people **need** food. Plants **need** water. Tom **needs** new gloves this winter. **needed, needing.**

neighbor A **neighbor** is a person who lives close to you. Our **neighbors** are working in their yard. **neighbors.**

neighbor

neighborhood   A **neighborhood** is the part of town where you live. There is a small park in our **neighborhood**. **neighborhoods.**

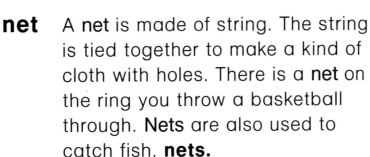

neighborhood

nest   A **nest** is a kind of home birds build. It is shaped like a bowl. **Nests** are made from straw, leaves, and other things. Baby birds live in **nests. nests.**

nest

net   A **net** is made of string. The string is tied together to make a kind of cloth with holes. There is a **net** on the ring you throw a basketball through. **Nets** are also used to catch fish. **nets.**

net

never   I have **never** met a monster. I hope I **never** will.

new   New means not old, or not used yet. We have **new** kittens at home. Her bike is **new. newer, newest.**

new

N | n

newspaper

newspaper A newspaper is sheets of paper printed with stories that tell what is happening. Many people read newspapers every day. **newspapers.**

next We will catch the **next** bus. Sit **next** to me.

next

nice Nice means good or kind. I had a nice time. It was **nice** of you to help me. **nicer, nicest.**

nickel

nickel A nickel is a kind of money. One nickel equals five cents. **nickels.**

night Night is the time between evening and morning. We sleep at **night**. Nights are dark. **nights.**

night

no   There are **no** oranges left. Just say **no** if you don't want to play.

no

noise   **Noise** means a sound we do not want to hear. The loud **noise** woke me up. **noises.**

noise

none   **None** of the children smiled. We wanted a cake, but the bakery had **none** left.

noon   **Noon** is 12 o'clock in the daytime. **Noon** is the middle of the day. We eat lunch at **noon.**

noon

N | n

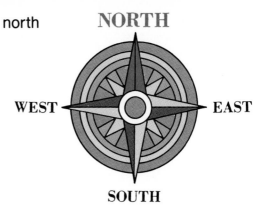

north

NORTH

WEST   **EAST**

SOUTH

nose

north   North is the direction opposite to south. If you look at the sun when it comes up, **north** is on your left.

nose   Your **nose** is in the middle of your face. **Noses** help us smell things. **noses.**

not   I am **not** surprised. It's **not** time to leave. Tom is **not** at home.

note   A **note** is a very short letter. My aunt sent me a **note** on my birthday. **notes.**

note

nothing   He saw **nothing** he wanted to buy.

now   Do the job **now**. We are leaving **now.**

number A number is a word that tells how many. 2, 9, and 15 are **numbers**. You use **numbers** in math. **numbers.**

number

nurse A nurse is a person whose job is taking care of sick people. Some **nurses** work in hospitals. Some **nurses** visit homes. **nurses.**

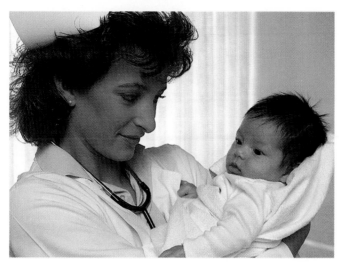

nurse

nut A nut is a seed or a dry fruit. **Nuts** have hard shells. Most **nuts** grow on trees. Some **nuts** are good to eat. **nuts.**

nut

Oo

oak   An **oak** is a kind of tree. We sat under the **oak** to get out of the sun. **oaks.**

oak

object　An **object** is something you can see or touch. A chair, a book, and a pencil are **objects**. How many **objects** can you carry in your pocket? **objects.**

object

observe　When we **observe** something, we look at it carefully and learn about it. We learn things from looking, listening, smelling, tasting, and touching. We use all our senses to help us **observe. observed, observing.**

observe

ocean　An **ocean** is salt water that covers much of the earth. Fish and whales are some animals that live in the **ocean**. Sea is another word for **ocean. oceans.**

ocean

o'clock　O'clock is a word we use to say what time it is. I eat my lunch at 12 **o'clock.**

octopus　An **octopus** is an animal that lives in the sea. It has a soft body and eight arms. **octopuses.**

octopus

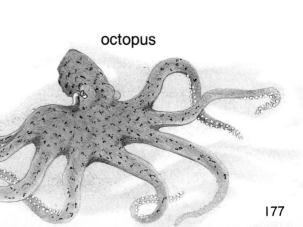

O o

off

of This book **of** mine is all about monsters. My toy dinosaur is made **of** plastic.

off I took **off** my coat. Jill pushed me **off** the swing. Mark's birthday is only three days **off**.

office An **office** is a place where people work. My mother took me to visit her **office**. **offices.**

office

often If something happens **often**, it happens many times. When we watch a movie, we **often** eat popcorn.

oil

oil **Oil** is a thick liquid. Some **oil** comes from under the ground. **Oil** helps machines to work. We cook with **oil** that comes from animals and plants.

old Someone who is **old** has lived for a long time. My grandmother is **old** and I am young. **older, oldest.**

old

on The paper is **on** the desk. The TV is **on.** I talked to Bill **on** the phone. I put my hat **on.**

on

once If something happens one time, it happens **once.** Jan has a piano lesson **once** a week.

onion An **onion** is a vegetable with a strong smell. The part we eat grows under the ground. **onions.**

onion

only Our dog is the **only** pet we have. Sue is the **only** girl on the baseball team.

only

O o

open

open   When you **open** something, people and things can get in or out of it. We **opened** the car window, and a butterfly flew in. That store **opens** at 9 o'clock. **opened, opening.**

opposite

opposite   When two things are as different from each other as they can be, they are **opposites**. Short is the **opposite** of tall. **opposites.**

or   I can play outside with my football **or** inside with my pet turtle. Hurry up **or** you will be late.

orange   **I.** An **orange** is a fruit that grows on a tree. **Oranges** are used to make **orange** juice. **oranges.**
2. Orange also is a color. Oranges and pumpkins are **orange**.

orange

order   **Order** is the way one thing comes after another in a special way. The children lined up in **order** of size. The words in the dictionary are in alphabetical **order**.

order

other The **other** children got dirty at the playground, but we did not. We'll go to the zoo some **other** day.

other

our **Our** garden looked beautiful, but their garden did not.

our

out The bird was not in its cage because it flew **out**. The firefighter put **out** the fire. Tom did not go **out** to play because he was sick.

outside Mom and Sue waited **outside** for the mail carrier to come. The **outside** of the carrot was dirty so we had to wash it.

outside

O|o

oven

oven An **oven** is the part of a stove that you use to bake things. The bread is ready to come out of the **oven**. **ovens.**

over Can you come **over** to my house after school? The robin flew **over** the trees. The milk ran **over** the edge of the glass.

over

owl

owl An **owl** is a bird with a big head and big eyes. **Owls** fly around at night. **owls.**

own **1.** When you **own** something, it is yours to keep. Do you **own** a bicycle? I **own** lots of books. **owned, owning.**
2. Something that is your **own** belongs to you. I want to have a room of my **own.**

Pp

pad A **pad** is a large, floating leaf. The frog sat on the lily **pad. pads.**

pad

P | p

page

page A **page** is one side of a sheet of paper. Turn the **page**. Books have many **pages**. **pages.**

pail

pail A **pail** is used to hold something in. Use a shovel to fill your **pail** with sand. **pails.**

paint

paint 1. **Paint** is a liquid used to color things. **Paint** comes in many different colors. Dad chose blue **paint** for my room. **paints.**
2. **Paint** also means to cover something with this liquid. Mom **painted** the kitchen yellow. **painted, painting.**

painter

painter A **painter** is a person who paints. Some **painters** paint houses. Some painters paint pictures. **painters.**

pair A **pair** is two things that go together. He lost a **pair** of mittens. **pairs.**

pair

P | p

pajamas Pajamas are clothes to sleep in. Pajamas have a shirt and pants. Sally bought yellow **pajamas**.

pajamas

pan A pan is something to cook food in. Use this pan to fry the eggs. **pans.**

pancake A pancake is a small, flat cake that is fried. Let's make **pancakes** for breakfast. **pancakes.**

pancake

panda A panda is a large animal. Pandas are black and white and look like bears. There are very few **pandas** alive today. **pandas.**

panda

pants Pants are clothes you wear on the lower part of your body. Some **pants** are long. Some **pants** are short.

pants

P p

paper

papa Papa is a name for father. **papas.**

paper Paper is used to write on and to make bags. It is made from wood. The pages of books are made of **paper.**

parade

parade A parade is a group of people walking together in rows down a street. Some **parades** also have people in cars. There were clowns and animals in the circus **parade. parades.**

parakeet

parakeet A parakeet is a bird with brightly colored feathers. It has a very long tail. Parakeets are often kept as pets. **parakeets.**

parent A parent is a mother or father. Paul's **parents** came to school. **parents.**

park
1. A **park** is an area of land with grass and trees. People can use **parks** for walking and playing. Some **parks** have playgrounds. **parks.**
2. **Park** also means to leave a car someplace for a time. Mother **parked** the car in the garage. **parked, parking.**

park

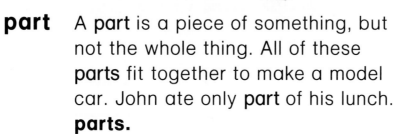

part

part
A **part** is a piece of something, but not the whole thing. All of these **parts** fit together to make a model car. John ate only **part** of his lunch. **parts.**

party
A **party** is a group of people having a good time. Alex went to the birthday **party**. **parties.**

party

pass
1. **Pass** means to go by. I **pass** the store on my way to school.
2. **Pass** also means to hand something from one person to another. Please **pass** the butter. **passed, passing.**

pass

P | p

paste

past **1.** Past means gone by or ended. Summer is **past**. This **past** weekend we went to the circus.
2. When you go **past** something, you go by it or beyond it. The children ran **past** our house.

paste Paste is used to make things stick together. Charles used **paste** to stick the pieces of paper together.

path

path A **path** is made when people or animals travel over the same ground a lot. **Paths** are not wide enough for cars. We like to walk on the **path** through the woods. **paths.**

paw

paw A paw is the foot of an animal that has nails. Cats and dogs have paws. **paws.**

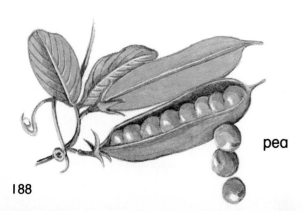

pea

pea A pea is a small, round vegetable. Peas are green and grow on vines. **peas.**

peach

peach　A **peach** is a round fruit that grows on trees. **Peaches** are juicy and have a fuzzy skin. **peaches.**

peanut　A **peanut** is a kind of seed that looks like a nut. **Peanuts** grow in shells under the ground. They are used to make **peanut** butter. **peanuts.**

peanut

peanut butter　**Peanut butter** is a food made from peanuts. **Peanut butter** is soft and is eaten in sandwiches.

peanut butter

peanu butte

pear　A **pear** is a sweet, juicy fruit. **Pears** are green or yellow, and grow on trees. **pears.**

pear

peek　**Peek** means to look quickly at something. Steve **peeked** at the presents in the closet. **peeked, peeking.**

P | p

pen   A **pen** is used for writing. **Pens** are often made of plastic. There is ink in a **pen. pens.**

pencil   A **pencil** is used for writing and drawing. A **pencil** must have a sharp point to write well. **pencils.**

pen

pencil

penny   A **penny** is a kind of money. It is another word for a cent. There are one hundred **pennies** in a dollar. **pennies.**

penny

people

people   Men, women, and children are **people.** There were many **people** at the picnic.

period   1. A **period** is one of the lengths of time in a school day. We will have a story in the next **period.**
2. A **period** is a dot at the end of a sentence. **periods.**

period

READING IS FUN.

person   A **person** is any boy, girl, man, or woman. **persons.**

pet   A pet is a favorite animal that you take care of. Liz has both a cat and a dog as pets. **pets.**

pet

phone   You use a **phone** to talk to someone who is in another place. A **phone** is another word for a telephone. **phones.**

phone

piano   A piano makes music. You play the piano with your fingers. **pianos.**

piano

pick   **1.** Pick means to choose. He **picked** the red wagon.
2. Pick also means to pull with the fingers. I **picked** some flowers in the garden. **picked, picking.**

picnic   A picnic is a party with a meal outdoors. People have **picnics** in the summer. **picnics.**

picture   A picture is something that you draw or paint. Jack drew a **picture** of his house. **pictures.**

picture

P | p

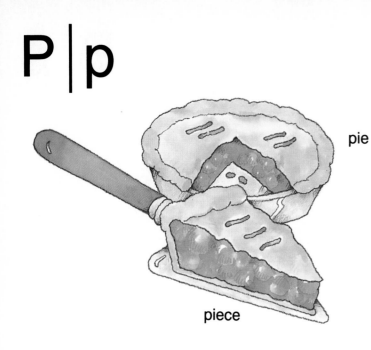

pie

piece

pillow

pilot

pig

pie   Pie is a kind of food. **Pies** are baked in an oven. Would you like some cherry pie? **pies.**

piece   A **piece** is one of the parts into which something is divided. A puzzle may have many **pieces.** Kim cut the pie into **pieces. pieces.**

pig   A **pig** is an animal with a fat body, short legs, and a curly tail. **pigs.**

pillow   A **pillow** is something soft you rest your head on when you sleep. **pillows.**

pilot   A **pilot** is a person who flies an airplane or helicopter. **pilots.**

pin   A **pin** is used to hold things together. It has one sharp end to stick through things. **pins.**

P | p

popcorn   Popcorn is a kind of corn that opens and makes a noise when you heat it. **Popcorn** is fun to make.

popcorn

porcupine   A porcupine is a small animal. Its back, sides, and tail are covered with sharp points called quills. **porcupines.**

porcupine

poster   A poster is a large printed piece of paper put up for everyone to see. Look at the circus **poster**. **posters.**

poster

post office   You can mail a letter at the **post office**. Mail carriers bring mail to you from the **post office**. **post offices.**

pot   A pot is used to hold things. Some **pots** are for cooking. Some **pots** hold plants or flowers. Dad made a big **pot** of soup. **pots.**

pot

potato   A potato is a vegetable. The part we eat grows under the ground. **potatoes.**

potato

197

P | p

pour

pour When you **pour** a liquid, it flows from one place to another. Cathy **poured** a glass of milk. **poured, pouring.**

practice Practice means to do something again and again. People **practice** in order to get better at doing things. Bill **practices** the piano every day. **practiced, practicing.**

present

present A **present** is something you give someone or someone gives you. Ann got a birthday **present** from her friend. **presents.**

pretend

pretend Pretend means to make believe that something is real when it is not. Let's **pretend** to be astronauts. **pretended, pretending.**

pretty

pretty Pretty means that something we see or hear is nice. Those flowers are **pretty.** I think the red flowers are **prettier** than the blue. **prettier, prettiest.**

prince   A prince is the son of a king or a queen. There are many stories about princes. **princes.**

prince   princess

princess   A princess is the daughter of a king or a queen. There are many stories about princesses. **princesses.**

print   Print means to write so that the letters do not touch each other. Jim printed his name at the top of the page. **printed, printing.**

print

prize   A prize is something you win for doing something well. Chris won a prize in the race. **prizes.**

prize

problem   A problem is something that needs to be worked out. What is the answer to this math problem? Making friends in a new town can be a problem. **problems.**

P | p

protect

project A project is a plan for doing something. Grace and her friends have a big project—they are building a tree house. **projects.**

protect Protect means to keep someone or something safe. **Protect** your eyes when you work with tools. **protected, protecting.**

proud Proud means thinking well of yourself or others. Ruth was **proud** of her team. **prouder, proudest.**

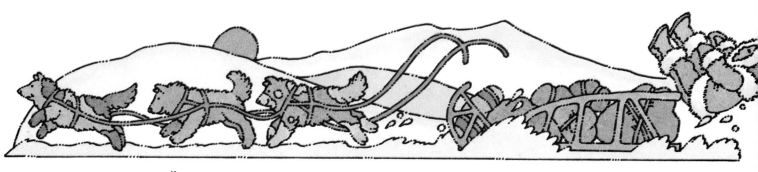

pull

pumpkin

pull Pull means to move something toward you. It is hard to **pull** weeds from the ground. The dogs **pulled** the sled a long way. **pulled, pulling.**

pumpkin A pumpkin is a large orange fruit. **Pumpkins** grow on vines. They are used for making pies. **pumpkins.**

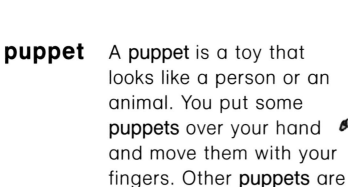

P | p

puppet   A **puppet** is a toy that looks like a person or an animal. You put some **puppets** over your hand and move them with your fingers. Other **puppets** are moved by strings from above. **puppets.**

puppet

puppy   A **puppy** is a baby dog. **puppies.**

puppy

purple   **Purple** is a color. It is made by mixing red and blue. Some grapes are **purple**.

purple

push   **Push** means to move something away from you. Dad **pushed** the door open. **pushed, pushing.**

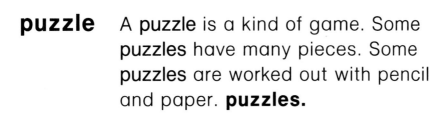

push

put   **Put** means to place or set something somewhere. She **put** her book on the table. **put, putting.**

puzzle   A **puzzle** is a kind of game. Some **puzzles** have many pieces. Some **puzzles** are worked out with pencil and paper. **puzzles.**

puzzle

201

Q q

quarter

quarter   A **quarter** is a kind of money. It is equal to 25 cents. Four **quarters** make one dollar. **quarters.**

queen   A **queen** is a woman who rules a country. **Queens** have great power. **queens.**

queen

question   A **question** is a sentence that asks something you want to know. When you ask a **question**, you want an answer. **questions.**

Is Jim home?

question

quick   When something is **quick**, it has great speed. The trip across the ocean by jet was **quick**. Kay gave a **quick** answer to the teacher's question. **quicker, quickest.**

quiet   **Quiet** means not noisy. Peter was **quiet** when he came home. A **quiet** room is best for studying. **quieter, quietest.**

quiet

quilt

quilt   A **quilt** is a soft cover for a bed. Sue's **quilt** keeps her warm at night. **quilts.**

Rr

rabbit   A rabbit is a small animal with long ears. Rabbits have long back legs and can hop very fast. **rabbits.**

rabbit

raccoon   A **raccoon** is a small animal with thick fur. Its tail is long, and has rings of a lighter color. **Raccoons** look for food at night. **raccoons.**

raccoon

race   **Race** means to run very fast. We **raced** to the corner. **raced, racing.**

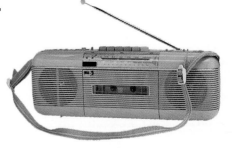

radio   A **radio** is something you can turn on and listen to. You can hear the voices of people far away by listening to the **radio. radios.**

radio

rain   **1.** The drops of water that fall from clouds are called **rain**. We shared an umbrella in the **rain**.
2. Rain also means to fall as drops of water. It has started to **rain**. **rained, raining.**

rain

rainbow   A **rainbow** is a curved band of many colors. It stretches across the sky. When the rain stopped, we saw a **rainbow** in the sky. **rainbows.**

rainbow

R | r

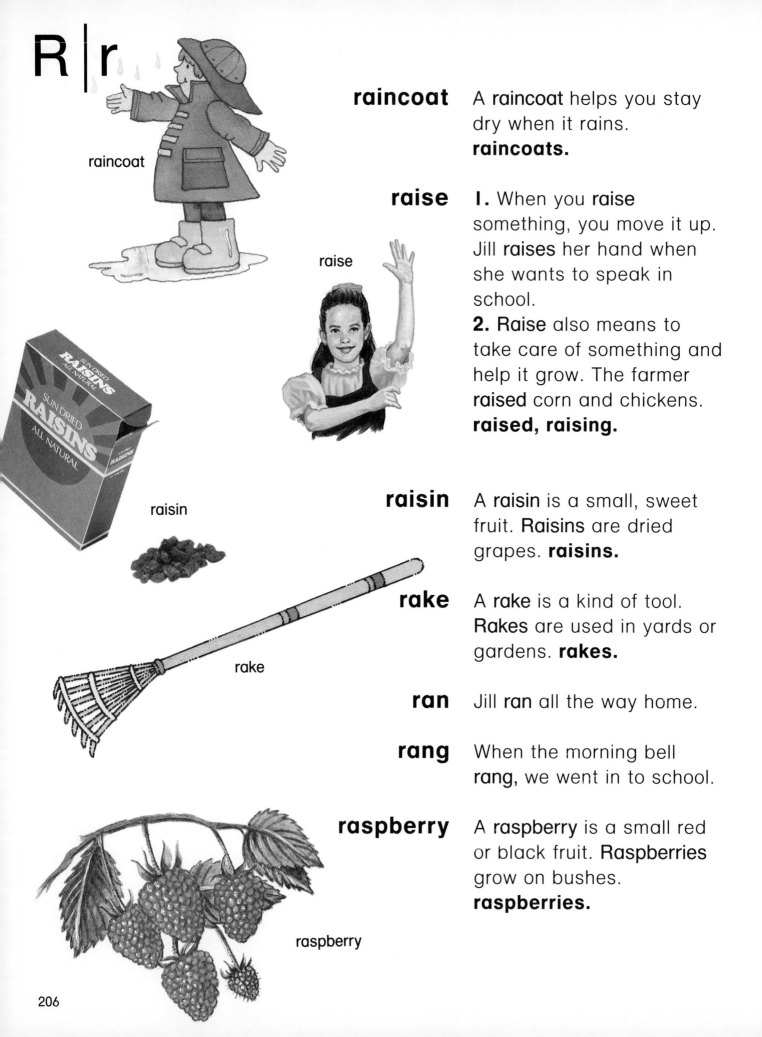

raincoat   A raincoat helps you stay dry when it rains. **raincoats.**

raincoat

raise   **I.** When you **raise** something, you move it up. Jill **raises** her hand when she wants to speak in school.
2. Raise also means to take care of something and help it grow. The farmer **raised** corn and chickens. **raised, raising.**

raise

raisin   A raisin is a small, sweet fruit. **Raisins** are dried grapes. **raisins.**

raisin

rake   A rake is a kind of tool. **Rakes** are used in yards or gardens. **rakes.**

rake

ran   Jill **ran** all the way home.

rang   When the morning bell **rang**, we went in to school.

raspberry   A raspberry is a small red or black fruit. **Raspberries** grow on bushes. **raspberries.**

raspberry

rat A **rat** is an animal that looks like a large mouse. **Rats** have long, thin tails. **rats.**

rat

reach **1.** When you **reach**, you hold out your arm and hand. Jim **reached** for the apple.
2. Reach also means to get to some person or place. The letter **reached** me last week. The river flows many miles to **reach** the sea. **reached, reaching.**

reach

read¹ **Read** means to look at and understand written words. Max is **reading** a story. **read, reading.** Read¹ sounds like need.

read¹

read² Max **read** a story to Ellen yesterday. Read² sounds like bed.

ready To be **ready** means to be all set to do something. Lee is **ready** for the party.

ready

R | r

real   Something that is **real** is true, not make-believe. Pandas are **real**, but unicorns are not **real**.

real

really   **Really** means truly. Is Dan **really** moving away? I **really** don't know.

reason   A **reason** explains why something happened. What is your **reason** for not coming to the party? **reasons.**

record

record   A **record** is something we can put on a special machine to play music. **Records** are round and flat. They are made of plastic. **records.**

rectangle

rectangle   A **rectangle** is a shape with four square corners. **rectangles.**

red

red   **Red** is a color. Strawberries are **red**. Milly's wagon is bright **red**.

refrigerator A refrigerator is used to keep food cold. **Refrigerators** are kept in the kitchen. **refrigerators.**

refrigerator

remember When you **remember** something, you keep it in your mind. Did you **remember** to bring your lunch? **remembered, remembering.**

report A **report** tells the facts about something. Kim's **report** was on Alaska. She gave her **report** to the class. **reports.**

rest

rest **I.** When you **rest**, you stay quiet. After playing hard, Meg **rested.** **rested, resting.**
2. **Rest** also means the part that is left. Would you like the **rest** of this fruit?

restaurant A **restaurant** is a place where you can buy a meal. **Restaurants** have many kinds of food to choose from. **restaurants.**

restaurant

R | r

return

return   Return means to bring back or to come back. Cal **returned** his library books, and then **returned** home. **returned, returning.**

review   When you **review** something, you look at it again. Please **review** your spelling list. **reviewed, reviewing.**

revise

revise   When you **revise** something, you change it. Ben **revised** his report by correcting all the mistakes. **revised, revising.**

rhinoceros

rhinoceros   A rhinoceros is a very large animal. It has thick skin and either one or two horns. Rhinoceroses eat grass and other plants. **rhinoceroses.**

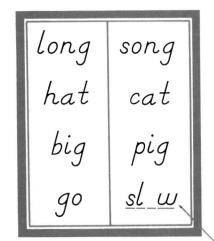

long	song
hat	cat
big	pig
go	sl_w_

rhyme

rhyme   Words that end with the same sound **rhyme.** "Long" and "song" **rhyme.** What **rhymes** with "go"? **rhymed, rhyming.**

rice

rich

rice Rice is a kind of food. It is often white, but can also be brown. **Rice** grows on a kind of grass.

rich **1.** Rich means having a very large amount of money. We read a story about a **rich** family.
2. Food that has a lot of butter and eggs is **rich**. The cake was so **rich** Jim could only eat a small piece. **richer, richest.**

rich

ridden Lynn had **ridden** her bicycle all morning.

riddle A **riddle** is a puzzle that asks a question. **Riddles** are often funny. Here is a **riddle**: ''Six people are under one small umbrella. Why don't they get wet?'' ''It isn't raining!'' **riddles.**

riddle

R | r

ride

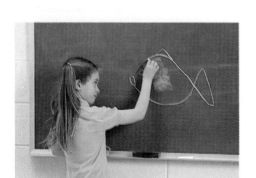
right

river

ride   When you **ride** something, it carries you along. Jill is **riding** her bike. Tom **rode** a horse. **rode, ridden, riding.**

right   **1.** When something is **right**, it is the way it should be. **Right** is the opposite of wrong. Tim had the **right** answer to the riddle.
2. Right also means the opposite of left. Stacey draws with her **right** hand.

ring¹   A **ring** is round and is worn on the finger. Beth wore her new **ring**. **rings.**

ring¹

ring²

ring²   **Ring** means to make a sound like that of a bell. I heard the telephone ring. **rang, rung, ringing.**

river   A **river** is a long stream of running water. It flows into a lake or ocean. A **river** has land on both sides of it. **Rivers** are bigger than streams. **rivers.**

road A road is a way to go between places. Cars and trucks are driven on roads. **roads.**

road

robin A robin is a bird. The front part of a robin is red. **Robins** are found in most places in the United States. **robins.**

robin

robot A robot is a machine that is run by a computer. **Robots** help people to do work. **Robots** can look like people. **robots.**

robot

rock Rock is very hard and is found in the ground. Mountains are made of rock. He threw a rock into the lake. **rocks.**

rode Jill rode her new bike. Tom rode a horse.

roll Roll means to move by turning over and over. Kate's ball rolled down the hill. **rolled, rolling.**

roll

R r

roller skate

roller skate

A roller skate is a shoe, or something you wear on a shoe, that has four wheels. **Roller skates** are used to skate on a floor, a sidewalk, or something else that is smooth. **roller skates.**

roof

roof The top covering of a building is the **roof**. Ken can see many **roofs** from his apartment. **roofs.**

room A room is part of the inside of a building. Each **room** has walls of its own. There are living **rooms**, dining **rooms**, and other kinds of **rooms**. **rooms.**

rooster A rooster is a kind of full-grown chicken. **Roosters** crow when the sun comes up each morning. **roosters.**

rooster

R | r

root   The part of a plant that grows below the ground is the **root**. Plants get food and water through their roots. **roots.**

root

rope   Rope is made of very thick string twisted together. **Rope** is used to tie things. **ropes.**

rose   A **rose** is a kind of flower. **Roses** smell sweet and are often red, pink, or yellow. **roses.**

rose

round   When something is **round**, it is shaped like a circle. Wheels are round. **rounder, roundest.**

row

row   When things are in a **row**, they are in a straight line. The cars are parked in a **row. rows.**

rug   A **rug** is something that covers the floor. **Rugs** can be large or small. **rugs.**

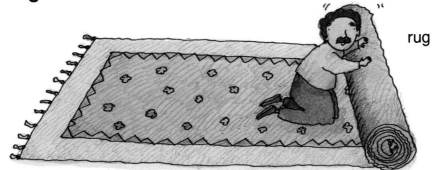

rug

215

R r

rule

rule **1.** A **rule** tells us what we must or must not do. It is a **rule** in our house that we put away our toys. **rules.**
2. Rule also means to have a lot of power over a country and its people. Many years ago a bad king **ruled** the land. **ruled, ruling.**

ruler A **ruler** is used to measure how long something is. **Rulers** also help to draw straight lines. **rulers.**

ruler

run When you **run**, you move your legs very fast. Jack **ran** after his dog. He has **run** after his dog many times. **ran, run, running.**

run

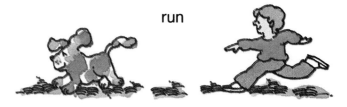

rung The bell has **rung.**

rush When you **rush**, you move in a hurry. Ken **rushed** out the door. **rushed, rushing.**

Ss

sad When you are **sad**, you feel bad about things. Jay was **sad** when his friend moved. **sadder, saddest.**

sad

S | s

safe

safe Safe means to be in no danger of harm. During the storm, Ben was **safe** at home. **safer, safest.**

safety Safety means freedom from harm. Rules about **safety** are important.

said She **said** she would help us.

sail

sail 1. A **sail** is a large piece of cloth used on some boats. **Sails** catch wind and help boats move. **sails.** 2. Sail also means to move across water in a boat. We **sailed** across the lake. **sailed, sailing.**

salt White grains of **salt** are added to food to make it taste better. **Salt** comes from the sea or the earth.

salt

salty When something is **salty**, it has a lot of salt in it. Tears are **salty**. This ham tastes **salty**. **saltier, saltiest.**

same When things are the **same**, they are alike. You and I have the **same** name.

same

sand **Sand** is made of tiny bits of broken rock. This beach is made of **sand**.

sand

sandwich A **sandwich** is a kind of food. It is made of two pieces of bread with meat, peanut butter, or other food in between. **sandwiches.**

sandwich

sang Mother **sang** a song to the baby.

sank

sank The boat hit the rock and **sank**.

sat Dad **sat** in his favorite chair.

sat

S | s

save   I. **Save** means to keep someone from harm. Nick **saved** his friend from being hurt.
2. When you **save** something, you keep it for later use. David is **saving** money for a bike. **saved, saving.**

save

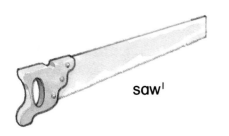

saw¹

saw¹   A **saw** is a tool used to cut wood. It has sharp metal teeth. **saws.**

saw²   Ann **saw** a beautiful red bird today.

say   When you **say** something, you are speaking out loud. Did Tom **say** he would be late? **said, saying.**

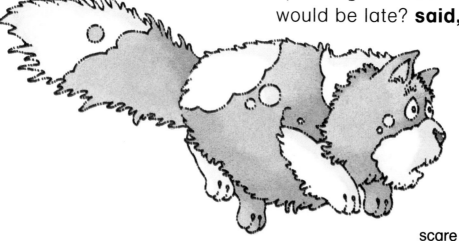

scare

scare   **Scare** means to make someone feel that something bad might happen. Storms **scare** me. **scared, scaring.**

school   **School** is a place where you learn things. We learn to read in **school.** **schools.**

school

science Science tells us why things are the way they are. We learn about the earth, the sky, animals, and people when we study science.

scientist A scientist is a person who tries to find out why things are the way they are. **scientists.**

scientist

scissors Scissors are used to cut things. A pair of scissors has two sharp edges that work together to cut paper or cloth.

scissors

sea The sea is salt water that covers much of the earth. Ocean is another word for sea. **seas.**

sea

seal A seal is an animal that lives in the sea. Seals have thick fur. **seals.**

seal

S | s

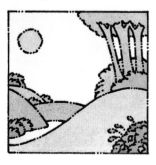

season　A **season** is one of the four parts of the year. The **seasons** are spring, summer, fall, and winter. **seasons.**

second¹　When something is **second**, it is the next after the first. B is the **second** letter of the alphabet.

second¹

second²

second²　A **second** is a very short period of time. Sixty **seconds** equal one minute. **seconds.**

secret　A **secret** is something you promise not to tell. The surprise party for Mom is a **secret**. **secrets.**

secret

see　When you **see** something, you look at it with your eyes. Did you **see** the red bird? **saw, seen, seeing.**

seed A **seed** is the part of a plant that grows into a new plant. If you put bean **seeds** in the ground, they can grow into bean plants. **seeds.**

seed

seem You **seem** sad. My dog **seems** to like that bone. **seemed, seeming.**

seen Have you **seen** the beautiful bird?

sell **Sell** means to give something in return for money. Dave will **sell** his bike for ten dollars. **sold, selling.**

sell

send **Send** means to cause someone or something to go from one place to another. I **sent** her a letter. Dad **sent** me out to play. **sent, sending.**

send

sense Sight, smell, taste, hearing, and touch are the five **senses.** Dogs have a very good **sense** of smell. **senses.**

sense

S|s

sentence

sentence

sent   Mom **sent** me to the store.

sentence   A **sentence** is a group of words that tells a complete idea. A **sentence** begins with a capital letter. It ends with a period, a question mark, or an exclamation mark. **sentences.**

set

sew

set   **1.** Set means to put something in place. **Set** the books on that table. **2.** Set also means to go down. The sun **set** at 8 o'clock. **set, setting.**

sew   Sew means to push a needle and thread through cloth. Pat likes to sew. **sewed, sewing.**

shadow

shadow   A **shadow** is a dark shape. It is made when something blocks the light. On sunny days, you can see your **shadow. shadows.**

224

shake Shake means to move up and down quickly. **Shake** the juice before you pour it. **shook, shaken, shaking.**

shake

shaken The medicine must be **shaken** before you take it.

shall I **shall** go to the party.

shape The **shape** of something is the way it looks. Wheels are round in **shape**. The cake was in the **shape** of a heart. **shapes.**

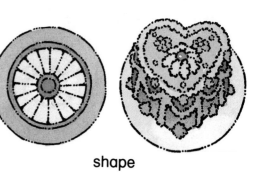

shape

share When you **share**, you let someone use something with you. The twins **share** a room. **shared, sharing.**

share

sharp Something that has a point or thin edge is **sharp**. This pin has a **sharp** point. **sharper, sharpest.**

sharp

she Who is **she**? **She** is my teacher.

S | s

sheep

sheep A **sheep** is an animal. Its thick, long hair is used to make cloth. Some farmers raise **sheep**. **sheep.**

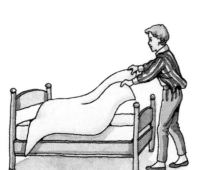

sheet

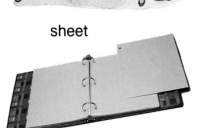

sheet 1. A **sheet** is a large piece of cloth used on a bed. A bed usually has a top **sheet** and a bottom **sheet**.
2. A **sheet** is also a piece of paper. I took a **sheet** of paper. **sheets.**

shell

shell A **shell** is a hard covering. Turtles and lobsters have **shells**. Eggs and nuts have **shells**. **shells.**

shine Shine means to give off a bright light. The sun **shines** brightest at noon. **shone, shining.**

ship A **ship** is a very large boat that travels on oceans or large lakes. People crossed the ocean by **ship** before there were planes. **ships.**

ship

shirt A shirt is a kind of clothing you wear over your chest and arms. Some **shirts** have buttons. **shirts.**

shirt

shoe A shoe is something you wear on your foot. Fran's **shoes** are blue, and Don's **shoes** are brown. **shoes.**

shoe

shone The sun **shone** brightly yesterday.

shook Kay **shook** the bottle.

shook

shop 1. A shop is a place where things are sold. There are two **shops** on our street. **shops.**
2. Shop also means to go to stores to buy things. I like to **shop** at the grocery. **shopped, shopping.**

shop

S|s

short

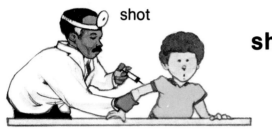

short

short   **1.** When something is **short**, it does not reach far from end to end. I live a **short** distance from school. Jill is **short** and her friend Lou is tall. **2. Short** also means not lasting long. We played for a **short** time after lunch. **shorter, shortest.**

shot

shot   When you are given a **shot**, medicine goes under your skin through a needle. People get **shots** so they won't get sick. **shots.**

should   You **should** drink milk every day.

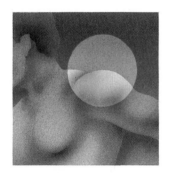

shoulder

shoulder   The **shoulder** is the part of the body between the neck and the arm. **shoulders.**

shovel   A **shovel** is a tool used to dig a hole or to scoop something up. I used a snow **shovel** to make a path to the garage. **shovels.**

shovel

show

show **I.** Show means to explain or point out something to someone. Kate **showed** me how to skate. **Show** us the toy. **showed, shown, showing.**
2. A **show** is something you watch on TV or at the movies. **shows.**

shown Max has **shown** us his new kite.

shut Shut means to close something or to put a cover on something. Ann **shut** the door. **shut, shutting.**

shut

sick

sick When you are **sick**, you do not feel well. Tim is in bed because he is sick. **sicker, sickest.**

side **I.** Side means the edge of something. A triangle has three **sides**. A square has four **sides**.
2. A **side** is also the part of something that is not the top, bottom, front, or back. The **side** of our house is near the fence. **sides.**

side

S|s

sidewalk

sidewalk A sidewalk is a place to walk on the side of a street. **sidewalks.**

sign

sign A sign tells you what to do or what not to do. Cars must stop at stop signs. **signs.**

sing When you sing, you make music with your voice. Marco sang a happy song. **sang, sung, singing.**

sink

sink 1. A sink is used to wash things in. Sinks hold water. Ben washed his hands in the sink. **sinks.**
2. Sink also means to go down or under. A rock sinks in water, but wood does not. **sank, sunk, sinking.**

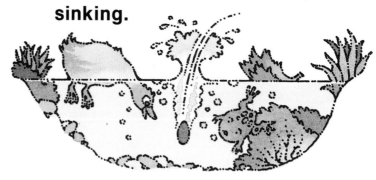

sink

sister Your sister is a girl who has the same mother and father that you have. Maria has a sister. **sisters.**

sister

sit

sit When you **sit**, you rest on the lower part of your body with knees bent. We **sat** in our chairs. **sat, sitting.**

size

size The **size** of something is how big or small it is. Dresses come in different **sizes. sizes.**

skate 1. A **skate** is worn on the foot. An ice **skate** has a sharp blade on it. A roller **skate** has wheels.
2. When you **skate**, you move along on ice skates or roller skates. **skated, skating.**

skate

skill A **skill** is something you learn to do by practice. Reading and writing are important **skills. skills.**

skill

skin **Skin** covers the outside of your body from head to toe. **Skin** helps keep body temperature even.

S|s

S | s

skirt

sky

skip Skip means to hop first on one foot and then on the other. When you **skip,** you can move from place to place. The children **skipped** to their places in line. **skipped, skipping.**

skirt A **skirt** is a kind of clothing that hangs from the waist. **Skirts** can be long or short. They are worn by girls and women. **skirts.**

sky The **sky** is the space far above you when you are outside. Today there was not a cloud in the **sky.**

sled A **sled** is used to slide on snow or ice. We used our **sled** after the first heavy snow this winter. **sleds.**

sled

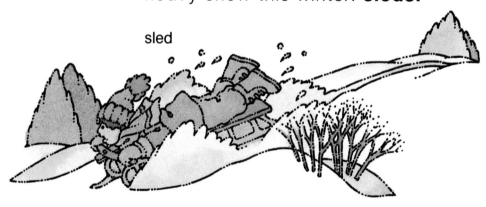

sleep

sleep 1. Sleep means to rest your body. Meg had a dream last night when she was **sleeping. slept, sleeping.** 2. Sleep also means the rest your body needs each night. I try to get eight hours of **sleep** every night.

slept   Joe **slept** through the storm.

slide   **1.** A **slide** is something to play on at a playground. You can slip down a **slide** or climb up it. **slides.**
2. Slide also means to move over something easily. Rose **slides** down the hill on her sled. **slid, sliding.**

slide

slip   **Slip** means to slide and fall. Mark **slipped** on the ice and broke his arm. **slipped, slipping.**

slip

slow   **1.** Something that is **slow** takes a long time. When something is **slow**, it is not fast. The **slow** runner lost the race. **slower, slowest.**
2. If you **slow** down, you take longer to do things. Al **slowed** down when Bob could not keep up with him. **slowed, slowing.**

slow

small   If something is **small**, it is not large. Chris's sweater has a **small** hole. **smaller, smallest.**

small

233

S | s

smell

smell   Smell means to use your nose to find out about something. You breathe in when you want to **smell** something. The freshly baked bread **smelled** good. **smelled, smelling.**

smile

smile   When you **smile**, the corners of your mouth turn up and you look happy. When Pam made a funny face, I smiled. **smiled, smiling.**

smoke

smoke   When something burns, it gives off **smoke**. Smoke is made up of the gases that come from the fire. The **smoke** helped the firefighter find the burning apartment.

snack

snack   A **snack** is a small amount of food eaten between meals. She had a **snack** after school. **snacks.**

snake

snake   A **snake** is a very long and thin animal. **Snakes** have no legs. They move by sliding along the ground. Some **snakes** are small, but some are very long. **snakes.**

ACHOO!

sneeze

sneeze When you **sneeze**, air comes out of your mouth and nose with a loud noise. A person with a cold often sneezes. **sneezed, sneezing.**

snow

snow **1.** Snow is frozen drops of water. Soft, white flakes of **snow** come down from the clouds in winter. The **snow** covered the grass in our yard. **2.** Snow also means to come down from the sky in the form of snow. It started to **snow** this morning. **snowed, snowing.**

so The dog seemed hungry, **so** we fed it. I was **so** tired I fell asleep.

soap We use **soap** to wash things and get them clean. We washed our hands with **soap** and water.

soap

soccer Soccer is a game played with a large ball. Players try to kick the ball down the field to win.

soccer

S | s

sock

sock A **sock** is clothing that covers your foot. Beth put on her **socks** and shoes. **socks.**

soft

soft **1.** Something that is **soft** is not hard or stiff. **Soft** things are nice to touch. My teddy bear is very **soft**. **2. Soft** also means not loud. Mother sang to the baby in a **soft** voice. **softer, softest.**

soil

soil **Soil** is the top layer of the earth. Plants grow in **soil**.

sold Dave **sold** his old bike.

sold

solid Anything that is a **solid** takes up space and has its own shape. It is not a liquid or a gas. Wood and ice are **solids**. **solids.**

S | s

some   Some of the children jumped rope. Some animals make good pets.

someone

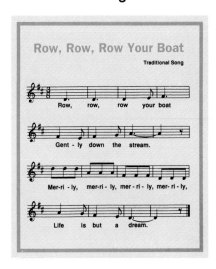

something

someone   Someone is at the door.

something   There is something in my soup.

sometimes   Sometimes I feel like playing with friends. Sometimes I feel like being alone.

son

son   A son is a boy child. A boy is the son of his father and mother. The Smiths have two sons. **sons.**

song   A song is music with words. You can sing a song. **songs.**

soon   Soon means in a short time. Soon it will be dark. **sooner, soonest.**

song

Row, Row, Row Your Boat
Traditional Song

Row, row, row your boat

Gent - ly down the stream.

Mer-ri - ly, mer-ri - ly, mer - ri - ly, mer-ri - ly,

Life is but a dream.

S | s

sorry

soup

sorry When you are **sorry** about something, you feel sad about it. Dan was **sorry** that he missed the baseball game. **sorrier, sorriest.**

sound

sound A **sound** is something you hear. He heard the **sound** of a bell. **sounds.**

soup Soup is a kind of liquid food. Mother made **soup** out of water, meat, and vegetables. **soups.**

sour Something that is **sour** tastes like lemon juice. It does not taste sweet. The cherries were **sour.**

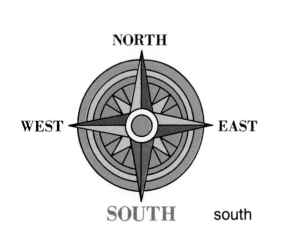

sour

south South is a direction. If you look at the sun when it comes up, **south** is on your right. **South** is the opposite direction to north.

NORTH

WEST   EAST

SOUTH   south

space 1. If there is room for something to fit, there is **space** for it. The puzzle piece was the right shape to fill the space. **spaces.**
2. **Space** is also the area around the earth. The sun and the stars are in outer **space.**

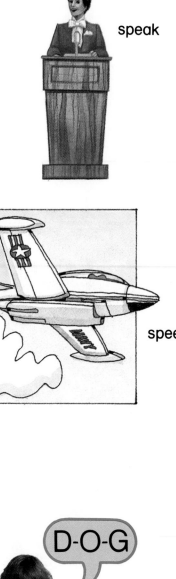

space

speak Speak means to say words or to talk. **Speak** louder so I can hear you. **spoke, spoken, speaking.**

speak

special Something that is **special** is unusual or different. Dad gave me a **special** present for my birthday.

speed

speed How fast something goes is its **speed.** The jet flew at a faster **speed** than the helicopter. **speeds.**

spell Spell means to say or write the letters of a word in order. We are learning to **spell** in school. **spelled, spelling.**

D-O-G

spell

S s

spend

spend
1. Spend means to use money to buy something. How much did you spend at the circus?
2. Spend also means to pass time in some place. Sue will spend a week at the lake. **spent, spending.**

spent
Jack spent five dollars at the circus. He spent Sunday at home.

spider

spider
A spider is a very small animal with eight legs. Spiders have no wings and are not insects. Many spiders make webs and catch insects in them. **spiders.**

spoke

spoke
Mandy spoke to our class today.

spoken
Father has spoken to the doctor about Jack's cold.

spoon

spoon   We use a **spoon** to eat food. Spoons have space at one end to hold the food. We eat cereal with a spoon. **spoons.**

sport   A **sport** is a game that needs skill and gives exercise. Basketball and soccer are sports. **sports.**

sport

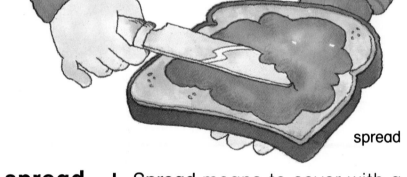

spread

spread   **1.** Spread means to cover with a thin layer. I **spread** the bread with butter.
2. Spread also means to pass on to other people. Sneezes and coughs spread germs. **spread, spreading.**

spring   Spring is one of the four seasons. It comes after winter and before summer. The trees get new leaves in the **spring.**

spring

S | s

square   A **square** is a shape. A **square** has four sides, all of the same length. **squares.**

square

squirrel   A **squirrel** is a small animal with a large, furry tail. **Squirrels** live in trees. They like to eat nuts. **squirrels.**

squirrel

stairs   **Stairs** are a group of steps that go from one floor to another. You can go up and down **stairs.**

stairs

stand   **1. Stand** means to be up on your feet, not sitting down. We **stand** up to read our stories to the class. **2.** When something **stands** for something else, it means the same. TV **stands** for television. **stood, standing.**

stand

242

star **1.** A **star** is something that shines in the sky at night. **Stars** are very far away from the earth.
2. A **star** is also a shape that has five or more points. My teacher drew a **star** on my paper. **stars.**

star

start **Start** means to begin to do something. I am going to **start** taking the bus. **started, starting.**

state A **state** is one of the parts of the United States. There are 50 **states.** John's family visited three **states** last summer. **states.**

state

stay When you are in the same place for a time, you **stay** there. I **stayed** with my grandmother last week. **stayed, staying.**

stay

stem A **stem** is a part of a plant. Flowers and fruit have **stems.** The trunk of a tree is a **stem. stems.**

stem

243

S|s

step

step
I. Each time you move your foot as you go from place to place, you take a **step**. It is just a few **steps** from here to the kitchen.
2. A **step** is also the place you put your feet when you walk up and down stairs. Billy reached the top **step** without falling. **steps.**

stick¹

stick¹
A **stick** is a long, thin piece of wood. We added **sticks** to the fire. **sticks.**

stick²

stick²
I. **Stick** means to push something sharp into or through another thing. I **stuck** my fork into the potato.
2. **Stick** also means to make things stay tightly together. John **stuck** the pieces of paper together with glue. **stuck, sticking.**

still
Ken is **still** watching TV.

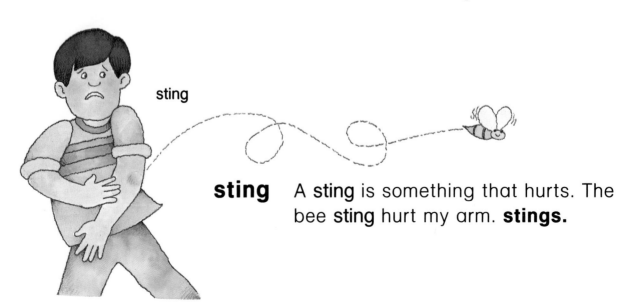

sting

sting
A **sting** is something that hurts. The bee **sting** hurt my arm. **stings.**

244

stomach
The food you eat goes into your stomach. Your **stomach** is like a large bag inside your body. **stomachs.**

stomach

stone
A **stone** is a small piece of rock. The children threw **stones** into the pond. **stones.**

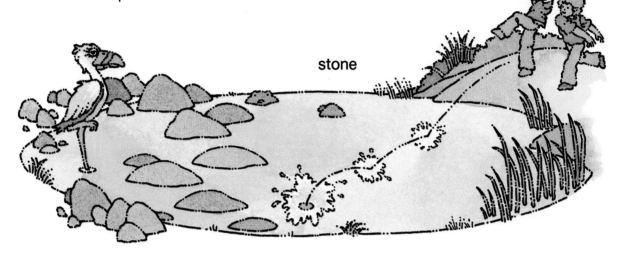
stone

stood
We **stood** up to cheer the team.

stop
I. We **stop** something when we don't do it any more. Jill asked her dad to **stop** smoking.
2. **Stop** also means to cause something not to move or continue. Drivers **stop** their cars at traffic lights. **stopped, stopping.**

stop

store
A **store** is a place to buy things. We drove to the toy **store. stores.**

S|s

storm

story¹

storm   A strong wind with heavy rain or snow is a **storm**. Some **storms** have lightning and thunder. **storms.**

story¹   A **story** tells about people and places and what happens to them. **Stories** can be make-believe or true. Do you know the **story** about the three bears? **stories.**

story²

story²   In a building, a **story** is all the rooms on one floor. Pat's house has two **stories. stories.**

stove

stove   A **stove** is used to cook or heat food. There are electric, gas, and wood **stoves. stoves.**

straight   Something is **straight** if it does not have a bend or a curve in it. Can you draw a **straight** line? **straighter, straightest.**

straight

stranger A **stranger** is a person you have not known, seen, or heard of before. Julie was a **stranger** until she met the kids in her class. **strangers.**

straw A **straw** is used to drink liquids. **Straws** are made of paper or plastic. **straws.**

straw

stream

stream A **stream** is running water. A small river is called a **stream**. Max caught a fish in the **stream. streams.**

street

street A **street** is a road in a city or town. I live on this **street. streets.**

stretch When you **stretch** something, you make it as long as it can be. The dog pulled my sweater and stretched it. **stretched, stretching.**

stretch

247

S | s

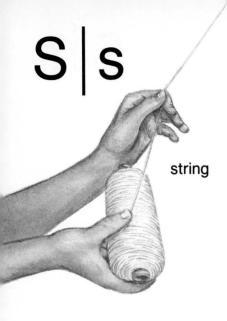

string

string
A **string** is a long, thin length of twisted threads. It is used to tie things. Ed bought **string** for his new kite. **strings.**

strong
Strong means not weak. A **strong** person can move heavy things. Mike was **strong** enough to move the table. **stronger, strongest.**

strong

study

stuck
Tim **stuck** his fork into the potato.

study
We **study** when we try to learn by reading and thinking. Liz **studied** her spelling. **studied, studying.**

subtract

subtract
Subtract means to take away. If you **subtract** two from three, you get one. **subtracted, subtracting.**

sudden
Something that happens fast is **sudden.** It is something you did not plan. The train made a **sudden** stop.

sugar Sugar is something sweet to put in food. This cake has **sugar** in it.

sugar

suit A **suit** is a set of clothes that go together. A man's **suit** has a jacket and pants. A woman's **suit** has a jacket and pants or a skirt. **suits.**

suit

summer Summer is one of the four seasons. It comes after spring and before fall. **Summer** is the hottest time of the year.

summer

sun The **sun** is a hot ball of gas. It is very far away from the earth. The **sun** gives us heat and light. The earth goes around the **sun.**

sun

sung Many songs were **sung** at camp.

sunk The rock has **sunk** to the bottom of the lake.

sunlight Sunlight is the light of the sun. **Sunlight** helps plants to grow.

sunlight

S | s

sunny   When the sun shines, it is **sunny**. I like **sunny** days. **sunnier, sunniest.**

sunny

sunshine   **Sunshine** is the light of the sun. I like to play outside in the **sunshine**.

sunshine

suppose   **1.** If you **suppose** something, you imagine that it is true. **Suppose** you go to the store. What would you buy? I **suppose** I'd buy toys.
2. If you are **supposed** to do something, you should do it. I am **supposed** to go home after school. **supposed, supposing.**

Surprise!

sure   When you are **sure** about something, you know you are right. Bob was **sure** that he had fed the dog. **surer, surest.**

surprise   **1.** Something that happens that you did not plan is a **surprise**. Tim loved the **surprise** he got for his birthday. **surprises.**
2. We **surprise** someone when we don't tell what is going to happen. We **surprised** Tim by giving him a new bike. **surprised, surprising.**

surprise

swallow   When you **swallow** food, you make it go from your mouth to your stomach. Barb **swallowed** the bread slowly. **swallowed, swallowing.**

swam

swam   We **swam** at the pool on Saturday.

swan   A **swan** is a large, white bird with a long neck. **Swans** live on lakes and rivers. **swans.**

swan

sweater   A **sweater** is a kind of clothing that keeps you warm. You can wear a **sweater** over a shirt. **sweaters.**

sweater

sweep   **Sweep** means to clean a floor with a broom or a brush. Greg **swept** the floor today. **swept, sweeping.**

sweep

251

S|s

sweet

sweet Something that tastes like sugar or honey is **sweet**. Most people like sweet food. **sweeter, sweetest.**

swept Greg **swept** the floor carefully.

swim Swim means to move in the water. People use their arms and legs to swim. **swam, swum, swimming.**

swim

swing

swing I. Swing means to move back and forth many times. The girls were **swinging** from the oak tree. **swung, swinging.**
2. A **swing** is something to sit on so you can move back and forth in the air. The **swing** at the playground is too high for me. **swings.**

swum We had **swum** in the ocean before.

swung Sue **swung** her arms as she ran.

Tt

table   A **table** has legs and a flat top. You can put things on a table. **tables.**

taco   A **taco** is a kind of food. **Tacos** are thin corn pancakes filled with chopped meat or chicken and other things. **tacos.**

taco

T | t

tail   A **tail** is the part of an animal's body farthest from its head. A fox has a furry **tail. tails.**

tail

take   **1. Take** means to get hold of something. **Take** an apple to eat. **2. Take** also means to carry. **Take** the sweater to the game with you. **took, taken, taking.**

taken   Jean has **taken** Al to school.

talk

talk   **Talk** means to speak. John is talking to Ruth. **talked, talking.**

tall

tall   When something is **tall**, it reaches a long way from top to bottom. Something **tall** is not short. The **tall** giraffe was as high as the tree. **taller, tallest.**

tan **1.** Tan is a color. It is a light, yellowish brown.
2. Tan also means to become brown by being in the sun. If you stay on the beach your skin will tan. **tanned, tanning.**

tan

tap Tap means to hit lightly. He **tapped** on the window. **tapped, tapping.**

tape

tape **1.** Tape is a long piece of paper, plastic, or some other material. Sticky **tape** is used to wrap things.
2. Tape also means to make a record on a special plastic tape. He **taped** the movie. **taped, taping.**

taste

taste You **taste** things with your tongue. When you **taste** something, you find out if it is sweet or sour or salty. **tasted, tasting.**

taught Peter **taught** me to play baseball.

taxi A taxi is a car with a driver. The driver is paid to take people from one place to another. **taxis.**

taxi

T t

teach

tear

teddy bear

teach   Teach means to help someone learn. She **teaches** people how to play the piano. **taught, teaching.**

teacher   A teacher helps people learn. Teachers work in schools. **teachers.**

teacher

team

team   A team is a group of people working or playing together. Sally is on the basketball **team. teams.**

tear   Tear means to pull something into pieces. The baby is **tearing** the newspaper. **tore, torn, tearing.**

teddy bear   A teddy bear is a soft toy bear. Many children like to play with teddy bears. **teddy bears.**

teeth

teeth   Teeth are part of your mouth. Your **teeth** help you bite and chew food. Each one of your **teeth** is a tooth.

telephone   A **telephone** is used to talk to someone who is in another place. When the **telephone** rang, Kim answered it, and it was Dad. **telephones.**

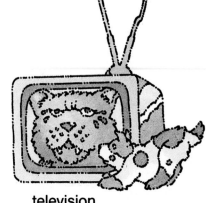
telephone

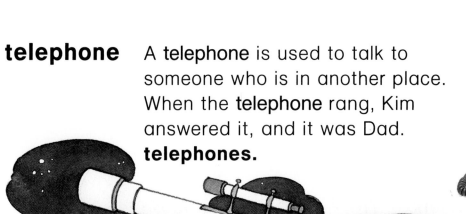
telescope

telescope   A **telescope** makes things that are far away seem near. You can look at the stars through a **telescope**. **telescopes.**

television   When you turn on a **television**, you can see pictures and hear sounds. You can watch shows and movies on television. **televisions.**

television

tell   Tell means to put into words, or to say. Gail likes to **tell** stories. **told, telling.**

temperature   Temperature means how hot or cold something is. The **temperature** outside is warm. **temperatures.**

temperature

257

T | t

tent

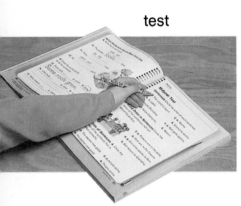

test

thank

tent A **tent** covers and protects you when you camp outside. It is a large piece of cloth held up by ropes and poles. We slept in a **tent** near the lake. **tents.**

test A **test** is a way to find out what you know or what you can do. **Tests** have questions to answer. **tests.**

than A mountain is bigger **than** a hill. Jane sings better **than** I do.

thank Thank you!

thank **Thank** is a word you use when something pleases you. I **thanked** Cathy for the present. You say "**thank** you" when something has been done for you or given to you. **thanked, thanking.**

that Who is the owner of **that** bike? I know **that** you are busy.

the   What is **the** name of your dog? **The** cat Betty found is black.

their   **Their** dog is black and mine has spots.

their

them   Ask **them** if they want to play outside. The books were new and I was careful with **them.**

then   Dad used to go running, and he was very thin **then.** We went skating, and **then** we had hot chocolate.

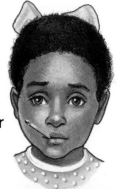

then

there   Sit over **there. There** are lots of people in the park.

thermometer   A **thermometer** is used to measure how hot or how cold something is. We looked at the **thermometer** to see how hot it was. Mom took my temperature with a **thermometer. thermometers.**

thermometer

T | t

these   Manuel read **these** books. **These** are his books and those are mine.

they   Luis and Maria came home late because **they** stopped to play.

thick

thick   When something is **thick**, it is not thin. A **thick** object is wide from one side to the other. The blue book is thick. **thicker, thickest.**

thin   **1.** When something is **thin**, it is not wide from one side to the other. Something **thin** is not thick. A sheet of paper is **thin**.
2. Thin also means having little fat on the body. John is very **thin**. **thinner, thinnest.**

thin

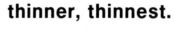

thing

thing   Don't leave that **thing** on the floor. Please put your **things** away. That is not a nice **thing** to do. **things.**

think 1. When you **think**, you use your mind. I had to **think** before answering the question.
2. **Think** also means to believe. Do you **think** it will rain? We **think** it might snow. **thought, thinking.**

third

third Third means next after the second. The **third** letter of the alphabet is C.

thirsty Thirsty means needing something to drink. The popcorn made me thirsty. **thirstier, thirstiest.**

thirsty

this This is my jacket and that is my brother's jacket. **This** year I am six.

those May bought **those** books. **Those** are her books and these are mine.

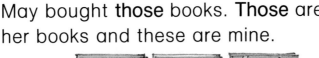

thought Jim **thought** about which record to buy. We **thought** it was raining.

thought

thread Thread is very thin string. You sew clothes with thread. **threads.**

thread

threw Kate **threw** the ball over the fence.

through The bird flew **through** the house. Are you **through** with your dinner?

through

throw Throw means to send something through the air. **Throw** the ball to me. **threw, thrown, throwing.**

throw

thrown He has **thrown** the ball already.

thumb

thumb The **thumb** is the short, thick finger on each of your hands. **thumbs.**

thunder

thunder Thunder is the loud noise that often follows lightning. My cat is afraid of thunder.

tie

tie   Tie means to hold something together by putting string or rope around it. She **tied** the package with white string. **tied, tying.**

tiger

tiger   A **tiger** is a large animal that looks like a cat. **Tigers** have yellow fur with black stripes. **tigers.**

time   Time is always going by. Seconds, minutes, hours, days, months, and years are ways we measure **time.** Clocks tell us what **time** it is.

time

tiny

tiny   Tiny means very small. Tiny bugs are hard to see. **tinier, tiniest.**

tip¹   Tip means the end part. She cut the **tip** of her finger. **tips.**

tip¹

tip²   Tip means to turn over. The boat **tipped** over. **tipped, tipping.**

T | t

tire   A **tire** fits around a wheel. **Tires** are filled with air. A car has four **tires**. **tires.**

tire

tired

tired   **Tired** means feeling worn out and ready to rest. Running made me **tired**.

title

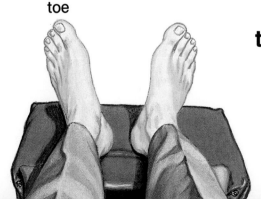

title   **I.** A **title** is the name of a book, poem, picture, or song. The **title** of this fairy tale is "Cinderella."
2. A **title** is also a name telling what a person is or does. "Mayor" and "prince" are **titles**. **titles.**

to   Are you going **to** the beach? What do you want **to** take?

today   **Today** means this day. **Today** I am going to the zoo.

toe

toe   A **toe** is a part of the foot. Each foot has five **toes**. **toes.**

together   Let's all go **together** to the lake.

together

told   My mother **told** me to be quiet.

told

tomato   A **tomato** is a round, red fruit. **Tomatoes** are juicy. They grow on vines. **tomatoes.**

tomato

tomorrow   Tomorrow is the day after today. We'll go shopping **tomorrow.**

tongue   Your **tongue** is part of your mouth. It moves and bends to help you say words. Your **tongue** also helps you taste food. **tongues.**

tongue

tonight   Tonight means this night. I am going to the movies **tonight.**

T | t

took

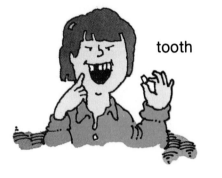
tooth

toothbrush

top¹

top²

too She felt **too** sad to go to the party. I was tired, and I was hungry **too.**

took My brother **took** us to school today.

tool

tool A **tool** is something that helps you do work. A saw is a **tool. tools.**

tooth A **tooth** is one of the hard, white parts in your mouth. You bite and chew food with your **teeth. teeth.**

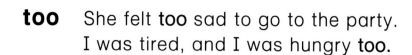

toothbrush A toothbrush is a brush used to clean your teeth. **toothbrushes.**

top¹ Top means the highest part. We saw the **top** of the mountain. **tops.**

top² A **top** is a toy that spins. The **top** went round and round. **tops.**

tore

T | t

tore I **tore** my jeans climbing a tree.

torn The picture was **torn** in half.

torn

touch Touch means to feel something with your hand. Chris **touched** the cat's soft fur. **touched, touching.**

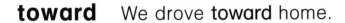

touch

toward We drove **toward** home.

towel A **towel** is a piece of cloth used to dry someone or something. Dry the dishes with a **towel**. **towels.**

towel

town A **town** is a large group of houses and other buildings. A **town** is smaller than a city. **towns.**

toy A **toy** is something to play with. Teddy bears and tops are **toys**. **toys.**

toy

267

T | t

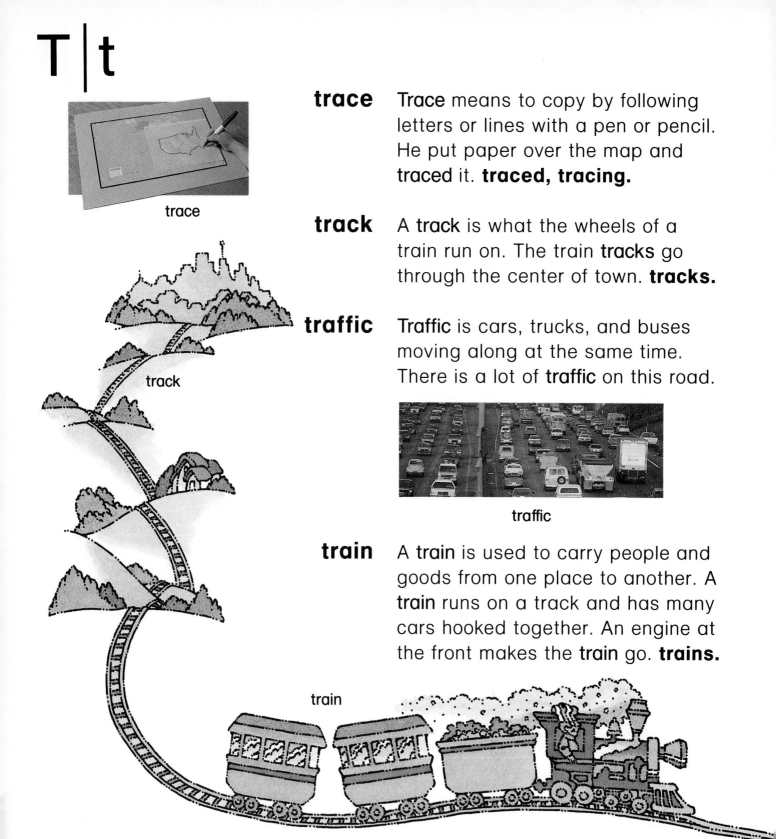

trace

track

traffic

train

trace Trace means to copy by following letters or lines with a pen or pencil. He put paper over the map and traced it. **traced, tracing.**

track A track is what the wheels of a train run on. The train **tracks** go through the center of town. **tracks.**

traffic Traffic is cars, trucks, and buses moving along at the same time. There is a lot of **traffic** on this road.

traffic

train A train is used to carry people and goods from one place to another. A **train** runs on a track and has many cars hooked together. An engine at the front makes the **train** go. **trains.**

travel Travel means to go from one place to another. They hope to **travel** next summer. **traveled, traveling.**

tree   A **tree** is a big plant. It has a trunk, branches, and leaves. Some **trees** have fruit that we eat. **trees.**

tree

triangle   A **triangle** is a shape. A **triangle** has three sides. **triangles.**

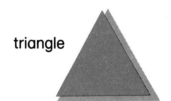
triangle

trick   A **trick** is something done to make people laugh or to fool them. A **trick** is also something you can teach an animal to do. Fran's dog can roll over and do other **tricks. tricks.**

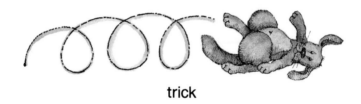
trick

trip   **1.** When you go on a **trip**, you travel from one place to another. Let's take a **trip** to the ocean. **trips.**
2. Trip also means to fall. I **tripped** on the rope. **tripped, tripping.**

truck   A **truck** is a machine that can carry heavy loads. It has a motor and wheels. **Trucks** are bigger than cars. **trucks.**

truck

T | t

true   True means right or correct. It is **true** that 4 and 6 are 10. A **true** story is not made up. **truer, truest.**

trunk   **I.** A **trunk** is a part of a tree. The branches and roots grow from the **trunk.** Trees have bark on their **trunks.**
2. A **trunk** is also a part of an elephant that looks like a very long nose. Elephants carry food to their mouths with their **trunks. trunks.**

trunk

try   Try means to set out to do something if you can. **Try** to hit the ball. **tried, trying.**

try

tube

tube   A **tube** is used to hold things such as toothpaste or paint. **Tubes** are made of plastic or thin metal. They have a cap on one end. **tubes.**

tulip

tulip   A **tulip** is a flower shaped like a cup. **Tulips** come in many colors. They bloom in the spring. **tulips.**

turkey A turkey is a large bird with brown or white feathers. **Turkeys** have long necks. **turkeys.**

turkey

turn **1.** Turn means to move around a center as a wheel does. The record kept **turning**. **turned, turning.**
2. Turn also means a chance to do something. It is her **turn** to read. **turns.**

turn

turtle

turtle A turtle is an animal with a soft body and a hard shell. **Turtles** live both in water and on land. **Turtles** can be small or large. **turtles.**

TV TV means television. I watched TV after dinner. **TVs.**

twin A twin is one of two children born to the same parents at the same time. Joe and Al are **twins**. **twins.**

twin

271

Uu

umbrella An **umbrella** is something you hold over your head to keep yourself dry when it rains. Mike's **umbrella** is made of cloth, but Ann's is made of plastic. **umbrellas.**

umbrella

272

uncle   Your **uncle** is your father's brother or your mother's brother. Your aunt's husband is also your **uncle**. **uncles.**

under   The ball rolled **under** the chair. Joe can buy the skates he wants for **under** ten dollars.

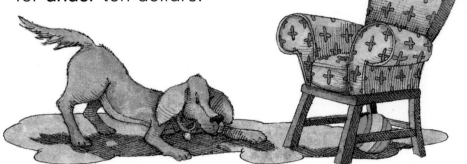

under

underline   When we draw a line under something, we **underline** it. The teacher asked us to **underline** the correct answer. **underlined, underlining.**

$$2 + 2 = ? \qquad 3\ 5\ \underline{4}\ 7$$

underline

understand   You **understand** something when you know what it means. Bob listened carefully so he could **understand** the directions. **understood, understanding.**

understood   Sue **understood** the rules of the game after Ann explained them.

understood

273

U u

unhappy

unhappy   Unhappy means sad. When Jim's best friend moved away, he felt unhappy. **unhappier, unhappiest.**

unicorn

unicorn   A unicorn is a make-believe animal. A unicorn looks like a horse with a long horn in the front of its head. **unicorns.**

unit   A unit is a special part of something. The first unit of our science book is about the human body. **units.**

until   Will couldn't wait until his birthday. He did not open his presents until his dad came home.

until

unusual

unusual   Something that does not happen often is unusual. It is unusual to see a horse wearing a hat.

up   The price of candy went up. The cat ran up the tree. We got up at seven o'clock. Your time is up now.

up

U|u

upon   Ann fell asleep **upon** her mother's lap. Once **upon** a time there was a dragon who was scared.

upon

us   Many of **us** played outside after lunch. The teacher called **us** when it was time to come inside.

use   Vera and I can **use** our tools to build a doghouse. Brian will **use** all the wood we have. **used, using.**

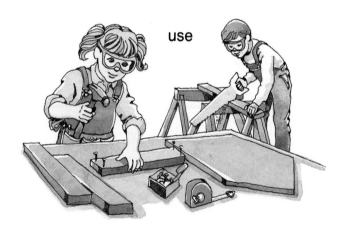

use

useful   When something is **useful**, it helps us. The hammer and saw were **useful** when we built the doghouse.

useful

usual   When something happens often, it is **usual**. Snow is **usual** here in the winter.

Vv

valentine   A valentine is a card or a small present that you send or receive on Valentine's Day. Amy received two valentines. **valentines.**

valentine

valley   A valley is the low area between mountains or hills. Rivers often run through valleys. **valleys.**

valley

van A **van** is a covered truck used to carry people or things. We used our **van** to go on a camping trip. **vans.**

van

vase A **vase** is used to hold flowers. Jan filled the **vase** with tulips. **vases.**

vase

vegetable A **vegetable** is a plant used for food. Peas, corn, lettuce, and beans are **vegetables. vegetables.**

vegetable

very Jerry was **very** hungry. He had a **very** large dinner.

village A **village** is a small town. There are few houses in a **village. villages.**

village   277

V | v

vine A **vine** is a plant that grows along the ground. Some **vines** climb up walls and fences. Pumpkins and grapes grow on **vines**. **vines.**

vine

violin A **violin** is used to make music. A **violin** is made of wood and has four strings. You push and pull a stick called a bow across the strings to make sounds. **violins.**

violin

visit

visit When you go to see places or people, you **visit** them. Ann wanted to **visit** her aunt. **visited, visiting.**

voice

voice Your **voice** is the sound you make with your mouth. You use your **voice** to talk and sing. **voices.**

Ww

wagon   A **wagon** can carry people or things. **Wagons** have four wheels. Sam's dog rode in the **wagon. wagons.**

wagon

W w

wait

wait Wait means to stay where you are. People **wait** for something to happen or for someone to come. We **waited** a long time for May and Billy to come. **waited, waiting.**

wake When you **wake**, you stop sleeping. What time did you **wake** up? **woke, woken, waking.**

wake

walk Walk means to move by putting one foot in front of the other. I **walked** to school. **walked, walking.**

walk

wall A wall is the side of a building or room. Ruth will paint the **walls** of her room blue. **walls.**

want

want When you **want** something, you would like to have it or to do it. I want a kitten. **wanted, wanting.**

280

warm   Warm means more hot than cold. It's a **warm** day. I felt **warm** by the fire. **warmer, warmest.**

warm

was   Her dog **was** gone. She **was** sad.

wash   Wash means to clean with soap and water. Joan **washed** her hands before lunch. **washed, washing.**

wash

watch   **1.** Watch means to look at something or someone. **Watch** how I do this. **watched, watching.**
2. Watch also means a small clock you wear on your wrist. **watches.**

watch

water   Water is the liquid that fills the ocean, rivers, lakes, and ponds. **Water** falls from the sky as rain. People and animals need **water** to live.

water

W | w

wave

wave　When the water in an ocean or lake rises and moves forward, it forms a **wave**. I saw the big **waves**. **waves.**

way　**1.** How something is done is the **way** it is done. This is the **way** I draw a tree.
2. Way also means the direction you follow to get to a place. Is this the **way** to Ben's house? **ways.**

we

wear

we　I met Jane, and **we** went skating.

wear　When you **wear** something, you have it on your body. **Wear** your brown jacket today. **wore, worn, wearing.**

weather　How it is outside is the **weather**. The wind, the air temperature, and how wet or dry it is tell us what the **weather** is like. The **weather** today is sunny and warm.

weather

web

web A **web** is made by a spider to catch insects for food. **Webs** look like nets made of very fine thread. **webs.**

week

week A **week** is a way to measure time. It has seven days. The days of the **week** are Sunday, Monday, Tuesday, Wednesday, Thursday, Friday, and Saturday. A year has 52 **weeks. weeks.**

weigh **Weigh** means to find out how heavy a person or thing is. I **weighed** the apples. **weighed, weighing.**

weigh

well **1.** **Well** means in a fine way. Kay does her work **well. better, best.** **2.** **Well** also means in good health. Ed felt sick, but now he feels **well.**

well

went Sue **went** to the store.

were They **were** cleaning the house. We **were** sorry it rained.

W | w

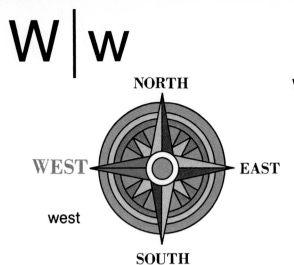

NORTH

WEST ● EAST

west

SOUTH

west   West is a direction. The sun sets in the **west**. **West** is the opposite direction to east.

wet   When something is **wet**, it is full of water. Lee's hair is **wet**, but Kate's is dry. **wetter, wettest.**

wet

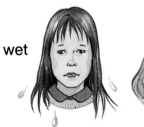

whale   A **whale** is a very large animal that lives in the sea. **Whales** are not fish. **whales.**

whale

what   What is his name? Liz doesn't know **what** to do.

wheel   A **wheel** is round. It turns around its center. **Wheels** help things move and work. Cars have four **wheels**. Bicycles have two **wheels**. **wheels.**

wheel

when   When are you leaving?

where   **Where** did you put your gloves? I know **where** they are.

which   **Which** book do you want to read? I don't know **which** way to go.

which

whistle   When you **whistle**, you make a clear, high sound by blowing air through your teeth or lips. Jim **whistled** for his dog. **whistled, whistling.**

whistle

white   **White** is a color. Snow is **white**.

white

who   **Who** is going to the ball game? Tell me **who** was at the party.

whole

whole   **Whole** means not having any parts missing. The **whole** class is here. There is only one **whole** apple left.

W | w

wide

wig

why   **Why** are you sad? Tell Mom the reason **why** you are sad.

wide   When something is **wide**, it is big from side to side. The road to town is **wide**. The ocean is very **wide**. **wider, widest.**

wig   A **wig** is a covering of hair for the head. She puts on a red **wig** when she dresses as a clown. **wigs.**

wild

wild   **Wild** means not raised or grown by people. **Wild** animals live in the forest. **Wild** flowers grow in the woods. **wilder, wildest.**

will   I **will** be able to go to the party. Sue **will** ask her mom to drive me.

win   You **win** when you are better than others at doing something. You **win** when you are the best. Our team **won** the game. **won, winning.**

win

wind   Wind is moving air. The **wind** blew leaves off the trees. **winds.**

wind

window   A **window** is an open space in a wall. **Windows** are made of glass and can be opened. A **window** lets light and fresh air into a building. **windows.**

window

windy   When it is **windy**, there is a lot of wind. It is **windy** at the ocean. **windier, windiest.**

wing   A **wing** is a part of a bird, insect, or bat. **Wings** move and are used in flying. **wings.**

wing

winter

winter   Winter is one of the four seasons. It comes after fall and before spring. Winter is the coldest time of the year.

W | w

wish Wish means to want something. He wished for a bike. **wished, wishing.**

wish

witch A witch is a make-believe person. In stories, witches sometimes fly on brooms. **witches.**

witch

with Do you want to go with us? I cut the meat with a knife.

without

without Don't go out without a coat.

woke She woke up early this morning. She was noisy and woke up the whole family.

woke

woken She has woken up early again.

wolf

wolf   A **wolf** is an animal that looks like a large dog. **Wolves** live together in large groups. **wolves.**

wolves   We heard the cries of the **wolves.**

woman   A girl grows up to be a **woman.** Girls grow up to be **women.** **women.**

woman

women   These girls will become **women.**

won   Who **won** the football game?

wood   The trunk and branches of a tree are made of **wood. Wood** is used to build houses and make paper.

wood

woods

woods   **Woods** means a lot of trees and bushes growing together. There are many kinds of trees in the **woods.**

W | w

work

worker

world

worm

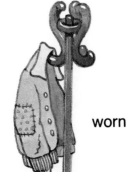

worn

word   A **word** is a sound or group of sounds that means something. People speak and write **words. words.**

wore   Jim **wore** new shoes to the party.

work   1. **Work** is a job you do. Driving a truck is hard **work.**
2. **Work** means to do a job. Lisa **worked** hard shoveling snow. **worked, working.**

worker   A **worker** is someone who works. Lisa is a good **worker. workers.**

world   The **world** is the earth and everything on it.

worm   A **worm** is a small, thin animal with a soft body. **Worms** have no legs and move by creeping. **worms.**

worn   He has **worn** that jacket often.

worse   Stan's cold is **worse** today.

worse

worst

worst   It is the **worst** cold he ever had.

would   **Would** you like some candy? She said she **would** come to the party.

wrist   The **wrist** is the part of the body between the hand and the arm. **wrists.**

wrist

write   **Write** means to make letters and words with a pen or pencil. Can you **write** your name? **wrote, written, writing.**

write

written   She has **written** a letter to her aunt.

2 + 2 = 5

wrong

wrong   **Wrong** means not right or not true. It was **wrong** of him to take my book. She gave the **wrong** answer.

wrote   Lynn **wrote** a poem.

wrote

My Parents
by Lynn
Roses are red,
Violets are blue,
I love my Mom
and my Dad too!

X x

X ray

X ray

An **X ray** is a picture that shows what is inside something. **X rays** can tell you if you have broken bones. They can tell you if you have any cavities in your teeth. My doctor took an **X ray** of my arm. **X rays.**

xylophone

A **xylophone** is used to make music. You hit the **xylophone** with wooden hammers to make different sounds. **xylophones.**

xylophone

Y y

yak A **yak** is a large animal with long hair. **Yaks** live in cold places. **yaks.**

yak

Y | y

yard

yard A **yard** is a piece of ground next to a house or a school. A **yard** may have a fence around it. Mother let us play outside, but we could not leave the **yard. yards.**

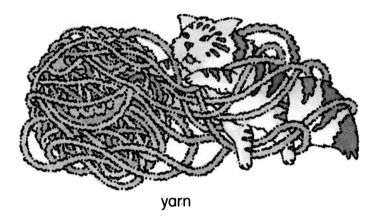

yarn

yawn

yarn Yarn is a kind of thread. It is used for knitting. Rosa lost her ball of **yarn** and her kitten found it.

yawn When you **yawn**, you open your mouth wide to get more air. People **yawn** when they are tired and need some sleep. **yawned, yawning.**

year

year A **year** is a way to measure time. A **year** has twelve months. The new **year** starts on January 1. Bobby is ten **years** old. **years.**

yell **I.** Yell means to cry out with a strong, loud sound. Nick **yelled** for help when he saw the fire. **yelled, yelling.**
2. Yell also means a strong, loud cry. Nick's **yell** made his mother call the firefighters. **yells.**

yell

yellow Yellow is a color. Lemons and butter are **yellow.**

yellow

yes When Sally says **yes** to something, she wants to do it. When Kevin asked her to come over, she said, "Yes."

yes

yesterday Yesterday is the day before today. We visited Grandpa **yesterday.**

you You have two sisters and I have one. **You** have more sisters than I do.

Y|y

young

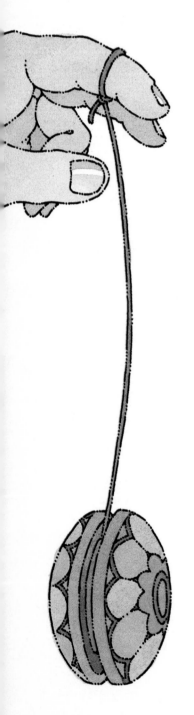
yoyo

young Young means to be in the early part of life. **Young** is the opposite of old. A puppy is a **young** dog. A baby is a **young** child. **younger, youngest.**

your **Your** toys belong to you. If you tell me **your** name, I will tell you mine.

yours This toy is mine, and that toy is **yours.** This pencil is his, and that one is **yours.**

yours

yourself Can you teach **yourself** the words to a song? Can you sing it all by **yourself?**

yoyo A **yoyo** is a toy made of two round pieces joined together. A string is tied to a **yoyo.** The **yoyo** goes up and down along the string. **yoyos.**

296

Zz

zebra A zebra is an animal that looks like a horse. Zebras have black and white stripes. **zebras.**

zebra

Z z

zero

zero   **1.** Zero is the number 0. If you put a **zero** after the number 1, you get the number 10. **zeros.**
2. Zero also means none at all. The score was nine to **zero**.

zip[1]   Zip means to move or act quickly. The cars **zipped** out of the parking area. **zipped, zipping.**

zip[2]   Zip means to close something with a zipper. Al **zipped** up his jacket before he went outside. **zipped, zipping.**

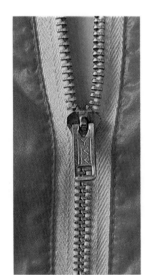

zipper

zipper   A **zipper** is used to hold things together. Sweaters, jackets, pants, and skirts can have **zippers**. Does your jacket have buttons or a zipper? **zippers.**

zoo   A **zoo** is a place where all kinds of animals are kept. People visit the **zoo** to see the animals. The **zoo** in our city asks us not to feed the animals. **zoos.**

zoo

Shapes

Find Out the Facts!

Can you find these shapes?

- ○ circle
- □ square
- ▭ rectangle
- △ triangle
- ☆ star
- ⬡ octagon

STOP

Numbers, Measurement

1	one
2	two
3	three
4	four
5	five
6	six
7	seven
8	eight
9	nine
10	ten
11	eleven
12	twelve
13	thirteen
14	fourteen
15	fifteen
16	sixteen
17	seventeen
18	eighteen
19	nineteen
20	twenty

12 inches equal 1 foot

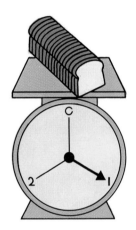
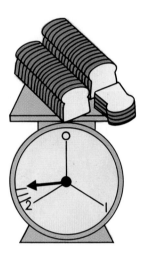

1 slice of bread weighs about **1 ounce**

16 ounces equal **1 pound**

1 kilogram is a little more than 2 pounds

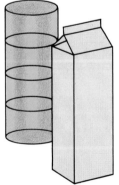

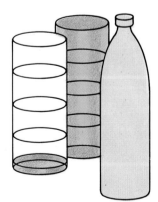

1 cup

1 pint
2 cups

1 quart
2 pints
4 cups

1 gallon
4 quarts
8 pints
16 cups

1 liter
is a little more than 1 quart

Parts of the Body

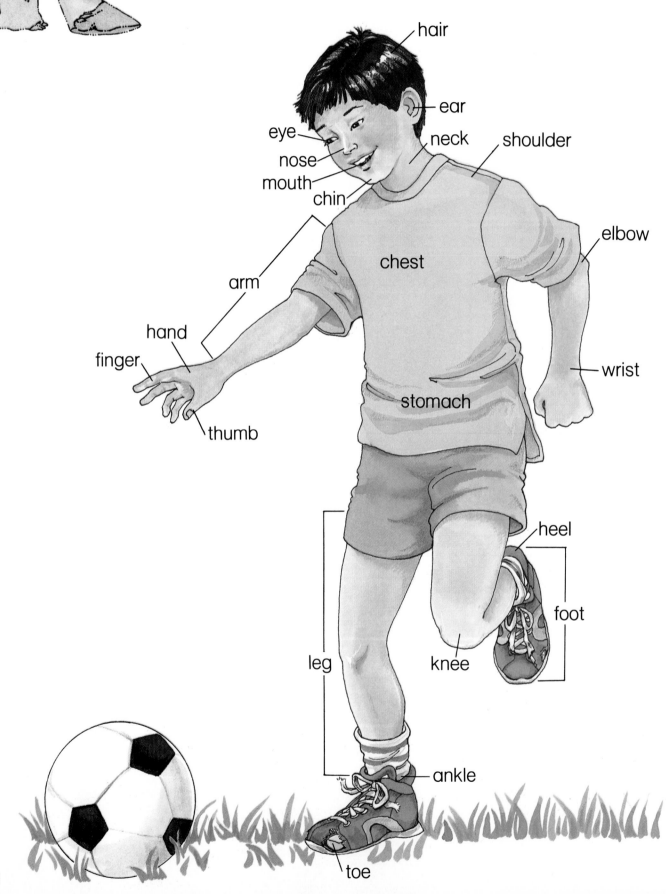

hair

ear

eye

neck

nose

mouth

chin

shoulder

chest

elbow

arm

hand

finger

wrist

stomach

thumb

heel

foot

leg

knee

ankle

toe

Healthy Snacks

Choose healthy foods when you want to eat a snack.
Stay away from foods that have a lot of salt.
Stay away from foods that have a lot of sugar.

Finding Places

	State	U.S. Post Office Abbreviation	State Capital
▪	Alabama	AL	Montgomery
▪	Alaska	AK	Juneau
▫	Arizona	AZ	Phoenix
▫	Arkansas	AR	Little Rock
▪	California	CA	Sacramento
▪	Colorado	CO	Denver
▫	Connecticut	CT	Hartford
▪	Delaware	DE	Dover
▪	Florida	FL	Tallahassee
▪	Georgia	GA	Atlanta
▪	Hawaii	HI	Honolulu
▪	Idaho	ID	Boise
▫	Illinois	IL	Springfield
▪	Indiana	IN	Indianapolis
▪	Iowa	IA	Des Moines
▪	Kansas	KS	Topeka
▪	Kentucky	KY	Frankfort
▪	Louisiana	LA	Baton Rouge
▪	Maine	ME	Augusta
▪	Maryland	MD	Annapolis
▪	Massachusetts	MA	Boston
▫	Michigan	MI	Lansing
▪	Minnesota	MN	St. Paul
▪	Mississippi	MS	Jackson
▪	Missouri	MO	Jefferson City

	State	U.S. Post Office Abbreviation	State Capital
▪	Montana	MT	Helena
▫	Nebraska	NE	Lincoln
▪	Nevada	NV	Carson City
▪	New Hampshire	NH	Concord
▪	New Jersey	NJ	Trenton
▪	New Mexico	NM	Santa Fe
▪	New York	NY	Albany
▪	North Carolina	NC	Raleigh
▪	North Dakota	ND	Bismarck
▪	Ohio	OH	Columbus
▪	Oklahoma	OK	Oklahoma City
▫	Oregon	OR	Salem
▫	Pennsylvania	PA	Harrisburg
▪	Rhode Island	RI	Providence
▫	South Carolina	SC	Columbia
▪	South Dakota	SD	Pierre
▫	Tennessee	TN	Nashville
▫	Texas	TX	Austin
▪	Utah	UT	Salt Lake City
▪	Vermont	VT	Montpelier
▪	Virginia	VA	Richmond
▪	Washington	WA	Olympia
▪	West Virginia	WV	Charleston
▪	Wisconsin	WI	Madison
▪	Wyoming	WY	Cheyenne

WASHINGTON

OREGON

NEVADA

CALIFORNIA

PACIFIC OCEAN

HAWAII

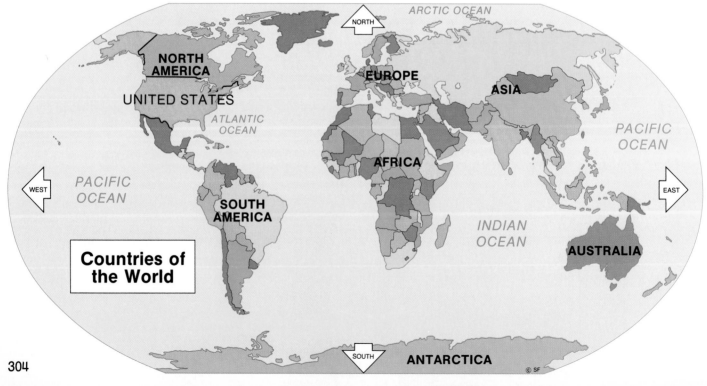

ARCTIC OCEAN

NORTH

NORTH AMERICA

UNITED STATES

ATLANTIC OCEAN

EUROPE

ASIA

PACIFIC OCEAN

WEST

PACIFIC OCEAN

AFRICA

SOUTH AMERICA

INDIAN OCEAN

EAST

AUSTRALIA

Countries of the World

SOUTH

ANTARCTICA

© SF

The United States

CANADA

MONTANA
NORTH DAKOTA
MINNESOTA
WISCONSIN
MICHIGAN
NEW HAMPSHIRE
VERMONT
MAINE
IDAHO
WYOMING
SOUTH DAKOTA
IOWA
NEW YORK
MASSACHUSETTS
RHODE ISLAND
CONNECTICUT
NEBRASKA
ILLINOIS
INDIANA
OHIO
PENNSYLVANIA
NEW JERSEY
DELAWARE
MARYLAND
Washington, D.C.
UTAH
COLORADO
KANSAS
MISSOURI
WEST VIRGINIA
VIRGINIA
ARIZONA
NEW MEXICO
OKLAHOMA
ARKANSAS
KENTUCKY
TENNESSEE
NORTH CAROLINA
SOUTH CAROLINA
TEXAS
MISSISSIPPI
ALABAMA
GEORGIA
LOUISIANA
FLORIDA

ATLANTIC OCEAN

ALASKA
CANADA
MEXICO

⊛ National capital

© SF

The World: Continents and Oceans

ARCTIC OCEAN
NORTH AMERICA
EUROPE
ASIA
ATLANTIC OCEAN
PACIFIC OCEAN
AFRICA
PACIFIC OCEAN
SOUTH AMERICA
INDIAN OCEAN
AUSTRALIA
ANTARCTICA

© SF

Calendar

Days of the Week

Sunday
Monday
Tuesday
Wednesday
Thursday
Friday
Saturday

Months of the Year

January
February
March
April
May
June
July
August
September
October
November
December

The name of the month is written here.

Month

Sunday	Monday	Tuesday	Wednesday	Thursday	Friday	Saturday
	1	2	3	4	5	6
7	8	9	10	11	12	13
14	15	16	17	18	19	20
21	22	23	24	25	26	27
28	29	30 Holiday				

The days of the week are listed here.

Each day of the week has a number. The numbers are in order.

Holidays happen on different days and in different months throughout the year. On some holidays, people do not go to work.

306

Holidays

January 1

New Year's Day is the first day of the new year.

January

Martin Luther King Day is on the third Monday in January.

February 14

On Valentine's Day, we send cards to people we love.

February

Presidents' Day is the third Monday in February. It honors George Washington and Abraham Lincoln.

March or April

At Easter, Christians mark the return to life of Jesus. It is a Sunday in March or April.

March or April

Passover is a Jewish holiday that comes in the spring. It lasts eight days. It marks the escape of the Jews from slavery.

May

Memorial Day honors Americans who died in war. It is the last Monday in May.

July 4

On Independence Day, Americans started a new country.

September

Labor Day honors working people. It is the first Monday in September.

October 12

Columbus Day honors Christopher Columbus. On this day in 1492 he first arrived in America.

October 31

On Halloween, people carve pumpkins and trick or treat.

November

Thanksgiving is the fourth Thursday in November. On this day we give thanks for what we have received.

December

On Hanukkah, the festival of lights, Jewish children give gifts and light candles.

December 25

Christians mark the birth of Jesus at Christmas.

Opposites

Can you pair the opposites in this picture?

high/low
above/below
on/off
hot/cold

thick/thin
clean/dirty
asleep/awake

more/less
empty/full
closed/open

over

under

happy

left   right

tall

short

outside   inside

big   little   top

bottom

small   large

soft

hard

in

out

wet   dry

over/under	in/out	big/little
happy/sad	left/right	top/bottom
small/large	tall/short	wet/dry
hard/soft	outside/inside	

Colors

red
+ yellow
= orange

yellow
+ blue
= green

blue
+ red
= purple

red

yellow

black

red

blue

brown

black
+ white
= gray

red
+ white
= pink

brown
+ white
= tan

Credits

The D'Nealian® Alphabet

a b c d e f
g h i j k l
m n o p q r
s t u v w x y z

A B C D E F
G H I J K L
M N O P Q R
S T U V W
X Y Z , ' . ?

1 2 3 4 5
6 7 8 9 10

The activities on these two pages encourage children to categorize, to compare and contrast, and to draw conclusions. They also foster creative thinking and independent learning. Not meant to be completed in one sitting, these activities can be done by one or two children alone, or with adult involvement. You might want to have on hand white glue, old magazines, paper, blunt scissors, paper plates, and markers or crayons. Then, step back and let the activities spark an interest in words.

☐ Can you name the opposites of the words below? If you need more help, look on pages 308 and 309.

awake and _____   hard and _____
big and _____   low and _____
cold and _____   tall and _____

☐ Listed below are five words. Put them in the order of the alphabet. If you are right, you'll make a sentence. Use this dictionary if you need to.

running   dogs   wild   big   like

☐ Look at the list of words below. They are in the order of the alphabet. One word has been left out. Between what two words does it belong?

eye
factory
helicopter   grandmother
important

☐ Look through this dictionary for the names of six foods that you like to eat. Write the words you find on a paper plate. Then look through old magazines for pictures of the foods that you have picked. Cut out the pictures. Glue them to your paper plate next to the words you have written.

☐ Pictures can tell you a lot. Can you match the words listed below with the correct pictures? Use the dictionary to check your answers.

brain   attic   elf   divide

☐ Look up the word <u>adult</u> in this dictionary. The word in **dark** type at the end shows you how the word is written when it means more than one. Look up the words below and make a list of the ways they are written when they mean more than one.

circus   city   child   fish   mouse

☐ Match the words below with their meanings. Check this dictionary to see if you are right.

leopard   aquarium   garden   haystack

1. This is where flowers or vegetables are grown.
2. This is a pile of hay that is stored outside.
3. This is a place where fish and other water animals are kept.
4. This animal looks like a large cat. It has spots.